UNLEASH YOUR FAITH – UNLOCK GOD'S POWER

JAMES DIXON, II

UNLEASH YOUR FAITH – UNLOCK GOD'S POWER
Copyright © 2009 by James Dixon, II

Unless otherwise noted, scriptures marked NASB are from the New American Standard Bible. Copyright © 1960, 1962, 1963, 1968, 1971, 1972, 1973, 1975, 1977, 1995 by The Lockman Foundation. Used by permission.

Scripture quotations marked KJV are from the Holy Bible, King James Version.

All rights reserved. No part of this publication may be reproduced, stored in a retrieval system, or transmitted in any form by means of electronic, mechanical, photocopying, recording or otherwise, except for the inclusion of brief quotations in a review, without prior permission in writing from the publisher.

ISBN: 978-0-9793192-7-3

Published by

LIFEBRIDGE
BOOKS
P.O. BOX 49428
CHARLOTTE, NC 28277

Printed in the United States of America.

Dedication

*This book is dedicated to a former slave,
Rev. Jack Henry Yates and those who founded
our church 135 years ago, and to those who by works
of faith, support and sustain it in this century.*

*I also dedicate these pages to Barack and Michelle Obama,
who first believed the Presidency could be achieved, and
now change has come to America and the world.*

Acknowledgments

*I give praise to my Lord, Jesus Christ!
What He has done for me, is doing in me
and done through me, amazes me!*

*To my beloved wife Tanisha and our children,
Mariah, Victoria, and James III, thanks for your endless
love and ceaseless prayers. I live to love you!*

*And to the many encouragers on this project,
who read, proofed, corrected and suggested...Thank You.
Especially I mention my family, Crystal Jackson, Evelyn
Banks, Terry and Karen Brown, staff members and our
literary team. Without your collective contributions
this work would only be an idea.*

May God's favor rest on you all!

"It is a great joy to see a book like *Unleash Your Faith – Unlock God's Power* available for God's people. As the author of the bestseller, *The Power of Positive Praying*, I can assure you that this book covers the waterfront of the priority of faith not only in prayer, but in the entire life of the believer. My friend James Dixon has 'nailed it.' This is not just a book about theory; it is a manual on how to do it. Our religion is appropriately called the Christian faith. It's all about faith. In these pages you are about to learn that and even more importantly, clearly understand how to practice it and receive the benefit. God bless you as you set out on this thrilling pursuit."

– Dr. John Bisagno, author and Pastor Emeritus, Houston's First Baptist Church, Houston, TX

Contents

Preface		6
The Evidence of Faith		8
Introduction		11
Part I Power Insights on Faith		13
Part II The Seven Power Keys of Faith		37
Power Key #1	Passages of Faith	37
Power Key #2	Principles of Faith	49
Power Key #3	Promises of Faith	55
Power Key #4	People of Faith	61
Power Key #5	Practices of Faith	72
Power Key #6	Process of Faith	77
Power Key #7	Proof of Faith	86
Part III The Seven Power Steps to Unleashing Your Faith		91
Power Step #1	Hearing	95
Power Step #2	Believing	103
Power Step #3	Speaking	109
Power Step #4	Desiring	123
Power Step #5	Praying	129
Power Step #6	Working	137
Power Step #7	Waiting	143

PREFACE

Every boy growing up in the hood encounters a bully or two. So did I. On one particular occasion, I had an episode with a dude I'll call Ray to protect his true identity. I am sure he, too, remembers the story.

I was about nine, Ray was at least four years older than me, and he was known for his exploits. He could intimidate you with some extremely harsh and terrifying words. So it was on this particular day when I became the target of his unprovoked maltreatment.

First came the talk, then the threats, and next he shoved me down a couple of times. Knowing that I needed an equalizer, I left the scene quietly, greatly embarrassed but determined that it was not over.

I soon returned to the street with my equalizer; my black Labrador retriever named Blazer, who absolutely loved me and my siblings. The look on my face not only said I was mad, but now I was armed and dangerous.

Ray was taunted by the boys in the neighborhood due to the fact I had returned with my dog. To protect his reputation he was forced to appear undisturbed, so he cursed at me and pushed me again. Blazer did not like this at all.

After a few ferocious barks, Ray began to run!

I held my loyal equalizer by his leash. Then, for some reason, I decided to let him go, and…well, it wasn't good. I can assure you that Ray never bothered little "Jimmy" again!

Sadly, far too many Christians are being bullied. We get pushed around in our families, finances, businesses, health, ministries, and careers. Most of us are afraid to pursue our dreams and visions because bullies rear their ugly heads and threaten to defeat us.

This book is written to help you realize that you have an equalizer called FAITH. It is your companion even when you are being tyrannized by life's circumstances and intentional opposition.

Like Blazer, your faith is barking, but you have to unleash it. When you do, you will put demons to flight. You will also gain the confidence to become, achieve, acquire, and do everything God has promised and purposed.

My friend, Tony Vega, who owns a superb Mexican restaurant in Houston, is an avid believer. He defines faith in one word, "JESUS!" And he is right. He is faith—the Author and Finisher.

When you unleash faith, you unleash Jesus and extraordinary things will happen. As you read this book, expect something awesome.

I'll see you in Heaven—if not before!

– James Dixon, II

THE EVIDENCE OF FAITH

This author can personally testify that what you are about to read really works.

When people visit our campus, which we call The Kingdomplex in Houston, Texas, they are amazed at what God has inspired us to accomplish. Touring the 55 acres of multi-faceted development points to the power of faith.

The Kingdomplex components consist of:

1 *The King's Dome*, a 90,000 sq. ft. worship and Christian education facility.

2 *Dominion Preparatory Academy* is a private, Christian, early childhood and elementary school.

3 *Dominion Academy Charter School*, a secondary school that provides a unique learning experience for 6th, 7th, and 8th graders. With a strong emphasis on business, economics, and entrepreneurship.

4 *Dominion Plaza*, a 38,000 sq. ft. retail service center.

5 *Dominion Estates I, II & III* is three subdivisions which we have developed from ground up consisting of 132 homes.

6   *Dominion Square Apartments:* 136 rental units.

7   *Dominion Park Recreational Complex* and more.

The principles and insights I share in this book have produced these visible results. Our church is not located in an affluent part of town or suburb. Our socio-economic conditions do not suggest that our campus should be comprehensive and expensive.

It has been our choice to defy the demographics and to be the change agent in our community. As I have said many times, "Faith has to defy some existing reality which it refuses to accept as permanent."

In our case, we refused to accept as permanent the rates of poverty, crime, rental versus home ownership rates, unemployment, education failure, and poor health.

We relocated to our present property when I was 23 years old. We had 250 people and less than $1,000 in the bank. The building we purchased cost approximately $1,000,000. The down payment was $90,000. Monthly payments were $8,014.92. We never missed one and the note was extinguished seven years early. It has been faith the entire way.

If you name it, we have probably faced it. We have never begun any project with all the answers, all the money, or all the support. Trust me. I have encountered more than my share of storms while on my way to the other side.

In my first book, *The Difference Is Vision*, I coined this definition: "Vision is a divinely inspired portrait of possibility, fueled by God's power, to accomplish God's purpose, through God's people for God's praise!"

The great news is that He is faithful and shows favor to those in faith. Even today, He continues to meet us at the point of our faith, with His favor. I have a dream now to build the vision center, a life and career development facility. I don't know where the money will come from. But I am praying and believing that somebody, somewhere, has the 2 million dollars we need—or access to it.

I can already see the young men and women in classes taught by our anointed team members with their special expertise and talents—including my wife teaching career readiness, my father teaching life skills, and I'm teaching the power of vision.

Through the eyes of faith, I can envision countless lives being changed for God's glory. Faith's transmission doesn't know reverse, only forward!

This book will teach you how, "to become a visible manifestation of the power of God in the presence of people."

INTRODUCTION

If you picked up this book out of curiosity, or simply to gain a little information on the subject of faith, let me suggest that you close these pages and give this to a friend.

What you are about to read is far more than surface knowledge on belief, hope, or expectation. It is designed to empower you, perhaps as never before, to step out on the waters of faith and do something truly extraordinary with your life.

This book is divided into three distinct parts. I will share with you *The Seven Power Keys of Faith*. I call them "keys" because they will unlock the doors of Heaven and allow you to start living the life God has planned.

You will also learn *The Seven Power Steps to Faith*, specific actions to take, both spiritually and physically, to make your walk with the Lord the exciting, rewarding adventure it was designed to be.

I want to give you the answers to these faith-building, life-changing questions:

- What are the essential *passages* in scripture to build my faith?
- What *principles* of faith does God want me to know?
- What are the *promises* of faith?

- Why should I surround myself with *people* of faith?
- What specific *practices* of faith should I follow?
- What is the *process* of building my faith?
- How can I experience the *proof* of the power of faith?
- What does *hearing* have to do with faith?
- How are *believing* and faith divinely linked?
- How does my *speaking* unleash faith?
- Is it scriptural to pray for what I am *desiring?*
- What is meant by *praying* in faith?
- What role does *working* play in our faith?
- What does God say concerning *waiting* in faith?

My prayer is that you will overcome doubt and disbelief and begin to operate with total trust in the knowledge that God's favor and blessings are yours.

At this moment, you may be facing a river that seems too wide to cross or a mountain too high to climb. The challenge may involve your family, your health, your finances, your business, or ministry. Step by step, I want to show you how to build and fortify your faith to the point that with God's help you can conquer life's greatest obstacles and seize profitable opportunities.

I believe you are ready to access the resources of Heaven. All things are possible when you learn to unleash the faith God has given you—and unlock His awesome power that is within you.

PART I

POWER INSIGHTS ON FAITH

Faith is an uncompromising confidence in God's ability, to perform His perfect will on my behalf, no matter what the opposition.

The reason I am thrilled you are reading this book is because I know how this teaching has transformed my life—and now I want to share it with you.

It is a composite of what I have learned through tedious study, 27 years of pastoring and a broad range of experiences, which includes many victories and some defeats. I know faith works!

By faith, I became a pastor at age 18 and have grown a congregation from 150 to 5,000. As we detailed at the beginning of this book, by faith, we have bought buildings, purchased land, and built a 90,000 square-foot worship complex called The King's Dome. By faith, we have developed and built three subdivisions. By faith, we have started and operate two schools. By faith, we have adopted a village in Africa through the Kingdom Builders Fellowship. By faith, I have fallen and gotten up. And by faith I stand awaiting the next victory!

You have a definite advantage in this world if you are a believer in the God of the Bible who reveals Himself in His son, Jesus Christ.

What is this advantage? It is accessing and triggering the power of God at will, through faith.

When we do this, we exercise God-given favor and become a force of faith in the world.

Unfortunately, there are far too many dissatisfied, frustrated, and unfulfilled believers. Most Christians live beneath their true potential. You may be one of them.

Why is this the case? Because too many people who claim to be born again are living in unbelief. I realize this sounds like a paradox, but it is nonetheless a reality.

A Common Deficiency

Let me call your attention to one of the "Seven Power Passages" I will explain later.

The father of a tormented, demon-possessed child brought his son to the Lord in search of a miracle. Jesus said to the man, *"All things are possible to him who believes"* (Mark 9:23).

This challenge exposes the man's deficiency. You see, it was not that the demons were so strong; rather the father's faith was so weak!

The father is not alone by any means. I've shared

company with him, more than I would like to admit. You probably have also.

You see, we often over emphasize the nature and size of our challenges, adversaries and obstacles. While doing this, we fail to focus on the true problem, our own faith deficiency.

On hearing the Lord's words, the boy's father immediately cried out to Jesus, "*I do believe; but help my unbelief*" (verse 24).

This is exactly what reading this book is purposed to do. It will help you conquer any amount of disbelief.

DON'T UNDERMINE YOUR POTENTIAL

Every time we operate in doubt we are disregarding the ability of the Almighty.

―――◆―――

If we are constantly complaining and discouraged, it means we are questioning whether or not the Lord is going to bring us through a particular situation. It also reveals a lack of confidence in the gifts and abilities we possess.

Just because we profess to be followers of Christ doesn't indicate we are operating and living in faith. Far too often we say:

- "I know God will supply all my needs." Then we worry and act like He may not.

- "I know He *wants* me to live in abundance." Instead, we pursue and settle for survival.

- "I know God *desires* my marriage to be happy and my family to be blessed." But we think realistically that doesn't happen anymore.

We continually question and doubt the Almighty. We claim our Heavenly Father owns the cattle on a thousand hills, however, we keep failing to access what is rightfully ours. Essentially we are repeating the same words as the father of the demon-possessed boy, "Lord, I believe. But please help my unbelief."

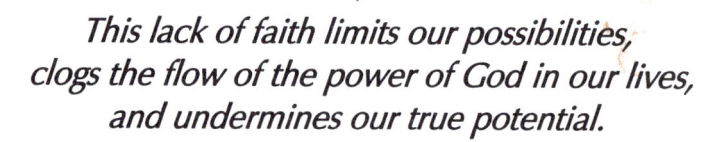

---◆---

This lack of faith limits our possibilities, clogs the flow of the power of God in our lives, and undermines our true potential.

This is why I believe the teaching you are about to receive is necessary for you personally and why it is equally relevant to the church collectively. If you want God's very best for your life, this book will teach you how to access it.

THE ALMIGHTY IS WITHIN YOU

To receive everything God has planned for us, there are three bedrock principles we must fully embrace:

1. God's unlimited power presently resides inside of every believer.

2. God's power is not subject to anything or anyone, at any time.

3. God's power is only accessed and activated when people operate in faith.

We must come to the place where we are able to declare, "All the God that God is, He is inside of me!" In other words, He is not more outside of you than He is within you.

Believers who understand this truth exude a level of confidence that causes some to envy them. It makes others nervous, and it causes the enemy to tremble.

When you not only believe this truth but begin to act upon it, you become distinguishable as a son or daughter of the Most High God. Why? Because you are able to have the Lord do a work in your life that unbelievers cannot experience.

So, when you release your faith, it unlocks the power of God to start flowing on your behalf. It creates a result that is obviously caused by the Almighty through you, proving to Christians and non-Christians alike that you are truly a child of God with favor.

Do You Have the Keys?

When I was a kid growing up, my parents owned nice cars.

I will never forget when I received my driver's license.

One of the ways I could prove I was my father's son was that I could ask for the keys to his automobile.

The point I am making is that if God is your Heavenly Father, but you never have use of His possessions, rise to a rewarding position, go any special places, and have no peace, people will begin to question whether or not you are really a member of His family.

Think about it. Your children look like they belong to you. Don't they?

―――◆―――

Once in a while you should be using something that belongs to your Father. Then people will remark, "They must be a person who has favor from God."

IS THERE A NOTICEABLE DIFFERENCE?

Your Heavenly Father wants to distinguish you from unbelievers, but in truth, there are too many Christians who are operating in unbelief. As a result, there are no signs, wonders, fulfillment, or joy attached to their lives. Not understanding why, they become dissatisfied, defeated and discouraged.

If you are a born again believer, yet there is no noticeable difference between your life today and how you lived before you came to the Lord, something is very wrong.

I've heard people comment:

- "I was struggling before I gave my heart to the Lord, and I am struggling now."

- "I was poor before I got saved, and I'm still living in poverty."

- "I keep hearing the preacher tell me what God wants to do in my life, but it never seems to materialize."

If these words mirror what you may have said, this book is for you! I want to show you from God's Word how to move from unbelief to faith and turn hope into reality. Don't give up on the Lord, the church, the Word or yourself. You are about to learn to use specific keys and take sure-fire steps that will literally *unleash* your faith—and as a result it will *unlock* God's power.

I believe you will experience a dramatic transformation from frustration to fulfillment.

DOES IT REQUIRE FAITH?

One of the purposes of faith is to open up the potential God's power affords. That is why Jesus said, *"And nothing will be impossible for you."* How do you know when faith is required? Faith is needed when the vision or goal you are seeking to accomplish is beyond your measurable capacity.

We measure our capacity in categories such as intellectual, physical, and financial.

Do I have enough knowledge? Do I have enough people? Do I have enough money? Do I have enough support?

If you always have enough capacity for the things you are pursuing, you will never use your faith.

I know many successful people who would agree with me. They are entrepreneurs, athletes, and ministers. Their stories are all different, but they are also similar. None of them ever had enough of everything necessary for their vision.

To be in a position to receive unlimited possibilities, stand firmly on these three important truths:

1. *Whatever I'm doing that doesn't require faith is a gross under-representation of what I could do, have or become.*

Regardless of how much I think about a particular objective, or even if I am actually working toward a specific goal, if I am not releasing my faith in the matter, I'm selling myself—and God—far too short. There is so much more I could seek the Lord for and accomplish, but faith is required.

2. *Whatever I'm doing that doesn't require faith is not God's best for me because without it I cannot access His highest and greatest blessings.*

Most of us were raised with these words ringing in our ears, "Do your best," or, "Be the best that you can be."

If my accomplishment is based solely on my intellect or ingenuity, I am only doing *my* utmost, not God's. It was a moment of personal revelation when I realized that the Father's goal for me was not simply that I was doing *my* best, but that *"Every good thing given and every perfect gift is from above" (James 1:17).*

At his best, Moses could not have crossed the Red Sea on dry land. At his best, Elijah could not have made fire fall from Heaven. At his best, David was not strong enough to kill Goliath. Faith activates God's power and enables us to perform at a level beyond our personal best.

3. Whatever I'm doing that does not require the exercising of my faith does not bring God glory.

If your achievement looks like it was all the result of your human effort, how can the Lord receive the honor due Him? Instead, you get the credit and God gets no praise.

God receives glory when you are seated in an office at your company that was reserved for another person—and your co-workers begin to wonder, "How did she get such a promotion?" He gets glory when you overcome what once dominated you.

The Lord receives glory when you purchase a home in a neighborhood that wasn't built with you in mind. He receives honor when an individual who knew you years ago didn't think you would make it—and you did!

Now those who looked down on you have to look up to you. People who live in faith become proven test cases of God's power. Only then does God receive the glory He is due.

UNLOCKED POWER!

What you are about to learn has *transformation* written all over it.

---◆---

If you begin to understand and practice these principles, you will never view God, yourself, or your life the same way again.

How will you know it is God's power that is being unlocked? I believe it will be similar to the way Jesus knew when a woman who had suffered with a hemorrhage for twelve years had approached Him. In a crowd that had gathered around the Lord, she touched the hem of His garment and was instantly healed.

Jesus turned and asked, *"Who is the one who touched Me?"* (Luke 8:45).

Jesus' question seemed a bit ridiculous. So many people had physically touched Him in this massive crowd, yet He asked, "Who touched me?"

Those in the throng didn't know, and the disciples did not know how to answer the question because of the large number of people pressing in around Him.

But Jesus continued, *"Someone did touch Me, for I was aware that power had gone out of Me"* (verse 46). This woman had reached out and touched Jesus with her faith!

Many people had made physical contact with Him, but nothing happened. Undoubtedly, some of them too had needs that could have been met.

The difference was this woman had reached out and touched Jesus with her faith. That is why His power was unlocked and her illness was healed.

When you learn to use your faith to touch the Lord, you will experience the transfer of His power into your life! Your active faith will get God's attention. You may be alone or in a crowd of others in a worship service. Everyone is in His presence, but you are the one who touches Him with faith.

CHANGE IS ABOUT TO HAPPEN

As you constantly expose yourself to the keys and steps you are about to discover, three important things will take place:

First: You will develop an <u>orientation</u> of faith.

When we face a problem or crisis, our initial response is in the flesh. We become fearful, angry, say the wrong things, and become discouraged. This is because our natural orientation is not one of faith but of flesh.

We are talking here about exchanging a flesh orientation for a faith orientation. One is natural, the other is spiritual.

The only way this can happen is by principles of faith sown into your heart, mind, and soul—which by the way is hard work.

You must do this daily with great discipline. You need to hear faith taught and see it lived. Saturate your world with faith.

When faith becomes your orientation, your responses change.

For example, if you suddenly receive a "pink slip" at work, or you are given a negative report from the doctor, or have a sharp disagreement with your spouse, what's your normal response? Would you become overtly angry, curse, and lose it? Would you cry, become nervous, anxious, and frightened?

Your responses come out of your subconscious mind. When you are filled with the Word you will intuitively think faith thoughts, speak words of faith, and take on a disposition of confidence.

―――◆―――

Developing a faith orientation will change how you respond to obstacles as well as opportunities.

When God presents you with a grand opportunity how do you typically react? Not only do big problems usually tempt us to respond in the flesh but big possibilities can have the same effect. Fear is fear, whether it is in response to something negative or positive.

A faith orientation will give you the confidence to process great possibilities. You will be able to see yourself in bigger, more prosperous and fulfilling places before you get there. You will be able to imagine yourself achieving and accessing potential greatness. If you can see it, you can believe it. If you can believe it, you can achieve it.

Second: You will develop an <u>outlook</u> of faith.

With your new faith orientation, the vantage point from which you view the problems or negative circumstance will be different. People in faith never put a period behind a problem.

———◆———

Your outlook of faith will cause you to believe and see problems as possibilities for God to demonstrate His power.

You will process everything you encounter in life through the lens of faith.

Tragically, most people are hindered by a negative outlook. They expect things not to work out for their good. They view the world, their relationships, their jobs and finances through negative lenses. I even know ministers whose outlook on their church is negative. Most people are pessimistic, skeptical, or cynical.

Men and women with a negative orientation are extremely difficult. They cannot do or support anything optimistically, and trying to build something positive with them is forever frustrating. Faith is perpetual positivity.

Third: You will learn to <u>operate</u> in faith.

All of these things will change the way you function. When challenges arise in your business, ministry, or family, you will praise God in advance for doors opened and needs met. People who operate in faith are different. Instead of responding to the problem with panic, they approach difficult situations with a calm assurance. It's called the peace of God which we are told surpasses human comprehension.

Whether the challenge is physical health, financial, or relational, people who have a faith orientation manage to operate in faith. Doing so keeps your mind open to hear God as He speaks wisdom into your situation. He already knows how to get us through every situation victoriously.

This is the opposite of an orientation of fear, which shuts down our ability to hear God and causes us to become vulnerable to the enemy. Rememberer, *"God has not given us a spirit of fear. But of love, power and a sound mind."*

When ruled by fear, one cannot love or be loved; one becomes weak and loses soundness of reason and judgment.

Faith keeps us available to hear God and to be at peace. This point is clearly seen in the episode where 5,000 men, not counting the women and children, were fed with the five loaves and two fish.

The enormity of the need (5,000 hungry men plus their families) did not make Jesus the least nervous. Neither did the fact that the only apparent resources were fish and loaves sufficient for a young boy's lunch. The disciples, on the other hand, were totally cynical, doubtful, and negative. They were fear stricken and fear guided. Therefore, they anticipated a fiasco.

Because they were in fear rather than faith, they perceived this would be a moment for grand defeat. Jesus anticipated a moment of grand success. Of course, Jesus was right.

My friend and a true man of faith, Dr. John Bisagno, has

said, "There's a difference between our apparent and God's actual."

Fear derives from only understanding what's apparent, but faith enables us to believe and access the actual, even when the actual is not visible....yet.

---◆---

It is important for every person in your impact circle to be united in faith, because those in fear will set you back.

Make certain these principles are taught and caught by every member of your family. This is especially important for married couples. It is also essential for church leaders, congregations, business partners, and teammates. To have one faction operating in fear and another operating in faith, jeopardizes the success and future of any group or organization. *"How can two walk together unless they agree"* (Amos 3:3).

Great and severe will be the consequences when one is in faith, but key partners are in fear.

In scripture, we observe this occurring in Numbers 12. The Israelites were set to enter the Promised Land which had been long awaited. Moses sent twelve leaders to explore the new territory. Ten returned gripped with fear while two returned pumped up with faith and ready to go. The problem was that the negative report was easier to believe because the unfavorable argument made sense. It appealed to the senses of the flesh.

Thus, the congregation wept, mourned, murmured and

complained. They even threatened to revolt against Moses, God's chosen leader who brought them through the Red Sea on dry ground. They preferred a leader who would lead them backwards to Egypt rather than one who could take them forward to Canaan. Why? Because going forward would require great faith.

Once the negative orientation that gripped the ten fearful leaders had spread throughout the congregation, chaos resulted. The cost was a forty year delay from entering their place of destiny and thousands of lives were lost.

Get it? That's forty years longer than necessary in an unfulfilling place. A generation later they finally crossed over the river Jordan by following people of faith.

Faith produces an uncompromising confidence in God's ability to accomplish His will on your behalf—regardless of what the situation looks like in the natural. Your key partners and those in your power group must also be in faith consistently.

A Visible Manifestation

One morning as I was driving, God spoke to me by His Spirit. It was so powerful that I wanted to pull my car to the side of the road, get out and start running down the street shouting!

Here is what rose up in my spirit. God said, "I want to make you a visible manifestation of my power in the presence of people."

My response was, "What?"

He repeated the words again, "I want to make you a visible manifestation of my power in the presence of people."

Then the Lord told me to speak this to those who will hear this word. It is what He desires for His children.

I do hope you will let this word simmer in your spirit. In fact, write it down and speak it aloud. This is God's intention concerning you: *"God is making me a visible manifestation of His power in the presence of people."*

This resembles what God told David in Psalm 23. He would prepare a table for him, even in the presence of his enemies (verse 5). Enemies, stay tuned!

When you begin to manifest God's power, those who know you—and even those who don't—will recognize that the Lord has done something supernatural on your behalf.

Why would He do this for you and me? Because this is how God receives glory. Today He is choosing you to become a visible manifestation of His power in the presence of people. He wants your family, finances, health, ministry and business to advertise His awesome power. Please believe and receive that appointment.

You may look at your present circumstances and mounting pressures and find it difficult to believe God wants to use you in this way, but it is true.

---◆---

The Lord desires more glory, and He is using you in the process.

COOPERATE WITH GOD'S PLAN

When you begin to live out the keys to faith, you become a visible, walking commercial, a living advertisement of the strength of the Almighty. This means when your enemies look at you they are going to see a picture of the power of God and won't be able to do a thing about it. Your enemies will walk away frustrated saying, "I tried to keep him down, but he got up anyway!" Remember Calvary, the tomb, and the resurrection of Jesus.

When this occurs, you are finally on your way to seeing God's vision and purpose for you become a reality. *"For I know the plans I have for you, declares the LORD, plans for welfare and not for evil, to give you a future and a hope"* (Jeremiah 29:11).

This is why it is so imperative to learn the keys to making this happen. We must use our faith to cooperate with what the Lord already desires to accomplish.

I pray you understand that you are not asking for or expecting that which God does not desire for you. This is what some people would have you to believe. To the contrary, it's His will for you to be a champion in life; He just needs you to use your faith to become a partner in His game plan for your victory. Say it now. *"I'm using my faith to become a visible manifestation of the power of God in the presence of people!"*

Now shout!

Faith is…A Victorious Response

I've been asked many times, "What is faith?" How do we use it in our lives?"

Thousands of words could be written in answer to the above questions, but let me share this working definition followed by three victorious faith responses:

> *Faith is an uncompromising confidence in God's ability to perform His perfect will on my behalf, no matter what the opposition.*

1. Faith empowers every believer's victorious response to opposition.

During the reign of King Saul, the entire army of Israel trembled in fear and anxiety because of the Philistine warrior named Goliath. Goliath defiantly stood in the valley, demanding, *"Choose a man for yourselves and let him come down to me. If he is able to fight with me and kill me, then we will become your servants; but if I prevail against him and kill him, then you shall become our servants and serve us"* (1 Samuel 17:8-9).

When this giant issued his challenges, the Bible records: *"Saul and all Israel…were dismayed and greatly afraid"* (1 Samuel 17:11).

In the middle of this scene, a young shepherd boy named David showed up. When he heard the defiance of Goliath, he said to King Saul, "I'm not afraid to fight him!"

Saul laughed at the idea of such a mismatch, but David assured him:

> *Your servant was tending his father's sheep. When a lion or a bear came and took a lamb from the flock, I went out after him and attacked him, and rescued it from his mouth; and when he rose up against me, I*

seized him by his beard and struck him and killed him.
Your servant has killed both the lion and the bear; and this uncircumcised Philistine will be like one of them, since he has taunted the armies of the living God.
And David said, "The Lord who delivered me from the paw of the lion and from the paw of the bear, He will deliver me from the hand of this Philistine" (1 Samuel 17:34-37).

This is faith talk in action—a believer's victorious response to opposition!

Be careful of the things you say in the face of opposition, a trial or crisis. You can no more control what's being said or done by others than David could control Goliath's vulgar threats or the fear talk of those around him, but you can control what comes out of your mouth. David spoke in faith. Why is this so important? Because even when others don't believe what you say, *you* believe what you say. What you say will either lock God out of your situation or invite God in.

As author Charles Henry Parkhurst expresses, "Faith is kind of a winged intellect. The great workmen of history have been men (and women) who believed like giants."

———◆———

It's not always the enemy who stands in your way. Often, you will meet good and decent people who infect you with doubts, fears, and pessimism. This is why your response is so vital.

Growing a ministry from 150 to over 5,000 has not been a piece of cake. Buying and developing nearly 60 city acres with schools, subdivisions, businesses and a myriad of programs has challenged us in every imaginable way. Without faith, it would be impossible. Trust me, I have had more than my share of external and internal opposition. Each new level and every new dimension reveals who is operating in faith and who is not. I have learned, and you must learn how to protect your mind and spirit from the well-explained, passionately-communicated fearful talk of people who may or may not be sincere.

2. Faith empowers every believer's response to obstacles.

One day, while on the shores of Galilee, Jesus said to His disciples, *"Let us go over to the other side of the lake"* (Luke 8:22). So they launched out.

At first it was smooth sailing, and Jesus fell asleep. Soon a major storm arose. Water began pouring in the boat, and they were about to capsize.

Frightened, the disciples woke Jesus, saying, *"Master, Master, we are perishing!"* (verse 24).

Jesus stood up and rebuked the wind and the surging waves—instantly, the tempest subsided and the waters became calm.

Then the Lord asked the disciples, *"Where is your faith?"* (verse 25).

They were amazed, saying to one another, *"Who then is this, that He commands even the winds and the water, and they obey Him?"* (verse 25).

The average person would panic in such a situation, but screaming and hollering won't tame the elements of your storm.

Faith alone seems impossible to those who don't possess it. Yet, as a born again believer you like Jesus can speak to the storm and it will obey your voice.

3. Faith empowers every believer's victorious response to opportunities.

Blessings appear in the form of opportunities. When Jehovah Jireh provides a door of opportunity we must be ready and willing to enter. Matthew 7:7 says, *"Ask and it will be given. Seek and you will find. Knock and the door will be opened."*

Many fail to walk through doors of opportunity because of fear. They fear not being qualified or they convince themselves, "I'm not from the right background. I don't think I can open such a business. I am not sure I can expand my territory, possess something awesome, or have the relationship of my dreams." These are fearful responses.

I have met people who pray for a blessing, then when it is about to happen, they shrink back in timidity.

The Bible tells us, *"Now faith is the substance of things hoped for, the evidence of things not seen"* (Hebrews 11:1)—but these "things" show up in the form of opportunities. They are the "rewards" for those who diligently seek Him (verse 6).

We must be willing to respond in faith as Caleb did. *"Give me this mountain"* (Joshua 14:12). He did not allow the challenge in the opportunity to damage his optimism. Although by the world's standards, he was too old to pursue such a task, Caleb conquered that mountain because he operated in faith.

---◆---

When you are offered a chance to succeed, don't turn it down. The Lord will give you what you need to take full advantage of the potential.

God declares, *"No weapon that is formed against you will prosper; and every tongue that accuses you in judgment you will condemn. This is the heritage of the servants of the Lord, and their vindication is from Me"* (Isaiah 54:17).

This promise and assurance is what gives me the courage to go where I have never gone, do what I have never done, have what I have never had, and become all I'm purposed to be. It causes me to have a victorious response to opportunities.

A verse of the sacred hymn says it best, "What have I to dread? What have I to fear? Leaning on the everlasting arm. I have blessed peace, with my Lord so near. Leaning on the everlasting arm."

The refrain goes on to say, "I'm safe and secure from all alarm."

THE ENEMY WILL FLEE

Remember, God's power presently resides in you and is

not subject to anything or anyone at any time. This means you do not have to worry about who is opposing you.

When you operate in faith, the power of the Almighty is accessed—and the enemy will have to move out of your way! In fact, your enemies will stumble and fall (Psalm 27). They don't all go away. If they did, they would miss your bountiful table which is being prepared for you.

Next, I will share with you Seven Passages that will empower you to unleash your faith and unlock God's amazing power.

I'm excited about the blessings awaiting you!

Part II

The Seven Power Keys of Faith

Power Key #1

Passages of Faith

"Man shall not live by bread alone, but by every Word that comes out of God's mouth."
– Jesus

There are specific passages of scripture that teach and explain faith. Although there are a plethora of books written on this topic, God's Word should be your primary source.

Let me recommend that you go on a faith diet, consuming

so much about faith that you think it even in your sleep. For example, make this commitment to yourself and to the Lord: "For the next 30 days I am not going to read anything that does not build or strengthen my faith."

You may check the headlines to find out what is happening in the world, but your intellectual intake should include no fiction, no romance novels, and no celebrity magazines! I promise, you will survive.

Instead, saturate your mind with specific scriptures and stories in God's Word dealing with faith. Read and consume as much about faith as possible, including inspirational works written by and about others.

To help you get going in the right direction, let me share what I call "The Seven Power Passages of Faith." There are certainly many others; the Bible is filled with them. But let's begin with these.

Power Passage Number One: Mark 9:23-24

And Jesus said to him..."'If you Can?' All things are possible to him who believes." Immediately the boy's father cried out and said, "I do believe; help my unbelief."

The purpose of faith is to open our hearts and minds to unlimited possibilities. *"All things"* means exactly what Jesus said—whatever you can believe God for, providing it doesn't conflict with His purpose.

Sure, moments of testing will arise, but they are opportunities to exercise our trust in God. How can we say we have faith when everything is running smooth and the skies are blue? It is only when our needs are beyond our own abilities that we can measure our faith.

In the case of the father who had a demon-possessed son, he was honest enough to admit his unbelief. Jesus used the situation to teach the man and us a lesson. The father had enough faith for this miracle but acknowledged not having perfect faith.

In the same way you are probably like me. I do have faith but it needs to be perfected. That is why we can believe God in some situations, but under different circumstances resort to fear and frustration. Some people can believe God for enough, but not *more* than enough. They can believe for a house but not a *nice* one. They can believe for little blessings but not *great* blessings.

———◆———

If you desire help with overcoming your unbelief, please keep reading and praying. As you conquer unbelief, more of God's best becomes accessible.

Power Passage Number Two: Mark 11:22-24

> *"Jesus answered saying to them, 'Have faith in God. Truly I say to you, whoever says to this mountain, "Be taken up and cast into the sea," and does not doubt in his heart, but believes that what he says is going to happen, it will be granted him.' Therefore I say to you, all things for which you pray and ask, believe that you have received*

them, and they will be granted you."

Jesus chooses mountain moving to illustrate the power a person in faith has. Not mountain climbing but mountain moving. That's completely different.

Notice, He chose no small object to make His point. Rather, He used an object that is awesome because of its size and because it is expected to remain stationary. A mountain is generally accepted as a fixed fact, a settled situation, and a permanent presence.

No scientist would offer a theory as to how a mountain could be relocated.

By using the faith command, Jesus says, we can move the mountains in our lives. The way we are to do this is by unleashing our faith through the use of our mouths.

What power the tongue has! As the Bible teaches, it commands life and death. When mountains block our progress we must remember how to unleash our faith and unlock God's power.

Later I will explain further how to utilize a faith command. When Jesus tells us to "say to this mountain, be taken up…" He is speaking of ordering it to move. It is the speech and tone of one who has authority over something.

If you are praying and believing for small things, you will only experience tiny triumphs. But as your faith increases, so will the size of your challenges and victories.

Do you have any situations in your life that seem unmovable? Do not accept any negative matter as a fixed and final fact. Regardless as to how long the challenge has remained, it is moveable.

◆

We need a conviction and a confession of faith.

How can we receive answers from Heaven? Jesus says that when you ask in prayer, *"believe that you have received."* In other words consider it already accomplished. As a result, *"they will be granted unto you."*

When you are asking God for something, you must believe you have already received it. Of course, we believe in our hearts. But we confess what we believe with our mouths. Read Romans 10:8-11.

Believing and confessing must always go together to bring a faith reality to total completion and manifestation.

Therefore, whatever it is that you are believing God about or for, you must confess it with your mouth.

The word "confess" is *homologeo* in Greek. So when we make a faith confession we are in accord with what we believe God will do based on what He has already said.

When Abram and Sarai accepted their new names from God they reintroduced themselves to the world. Of course their new names were Abraham, father of many nations. And Sarah, mother of princes. Each time they spoke of themselves or of each other, they made a faith confession. It was all day, every day.

And it came to pass.

Power Passage Number Three: Hebrews 11:1,6

"Now faith is the substance of things hoped for, the

evidence of things not seen...But without faith it is impossible to please Him: for He that cometh to God must believe that He is, and that He is a rewarder of them that diligently seek Him" (KJV).

───◆───
Hope is an unwavering expectation, which does not require tangible evidence.

Do you really believe the Lord is going to reward you? If you do, it will begin to show in your disposition. You'll have a look of expectation on your face.

Early one morning, a friend asked me, "How are you doing?"

I replied, "Victoriously well" which is my normal response to that question.

He commented, "How can you say that when you haven't really started your day?"

I told him, "I know even before the sun rises; I am going to have another victory under my belt."

I literally wake up believing that. By faith, I see the evidence coming my way; and the Lord *does* reward me!

Many people wake up each day expecting defeat. How tragic! Fear and faith are both choices. I choose faith. And I choose it every day of my life. Sometimes it needs to be an hourly decision. This is an attitude of faith, and one that pleases God. So much so that He is inspired to reward it whenever, wherever, and for whomever.

To unleash your faith you must have something specific for which you are hoping. Don't go through life, not even another day, without deciding on a thing to hope and believe God for. It can be a healed relationship, increased finances, a thriving ministry, a successful career, or something else that's wonderful. But please have an object for your faith. And remember, the proof that it will happen is not visible. It's your <u>faith</u>!

Power Passage Number Four: Romans 10:17

"So then faith cometh by hearing, and hearing by the word of God" (KJV).

Faith is Kingdom currency—which we only receive by one means, by hearing—and hearing comes from the Word.

Because of our capitalistic orientation, we think of money as the only medium of exchange. But cash is just one form of currency. For example, your good name is also currency, because with the right reputation doors will open wide for you.

When you study God's Word you learn that faith is more valuable than any earthly asset, because it will bring you what money can't buy. Wealth cannot purchase health or peace of mind at any price. You can pay a doctor with money but you can't purchase healing.

———◆———

You can use your faith to attain finances, but you can't use your finances to purchase faith.

It's amazing what people will do for money. They will spend years in higher education, toil ten or twelve hours a day, and even work around those they don't like. Most people will do whatever it takes to earn a paycheck or gain more money; but only a few will apply the discipline necessary to increase their faith.

Faith is Kingdom currency. So the question is: What are you willing to go through to obtain more of it?

In France, the currency is the Euro. In Mexico, it's the Peso. In Japan, it's the Yen. In the U.S., it's the Dollar. In Britain, it's the Pound. But in God's Kingdom the currency is FAITH!

I hope you are not one of those who think hearing the Word in a worship service is wasted time.

Remember, faith comes by hearing. So how many hours this week will you spend in the Word to hear God's voice?

Power Passage Number Five:
2 Corinthians 5:7

"...for we walk by faith, not by sight."

"Seeing is believing." Oh how I pity the persons for whom this is true. Just think of all they will never believe!

They cannot believe the Bible. They cannot believe Jesus' virgin birth, death on the cross or resurrection from the dead. They cannot believe in Heaven and eternal life.

These are all truths that must be accepted by faith. The word for "sight" in this text means to perceive through the senses or to understand by way of reason. But as brilliant as man is, we are grossly incapable of perceiving and understanding so much.

And to rely strictly on our limited capacity puts us at a severe disadvantage. Too often, the visible evidence is negative and discouraging. But faith, our God sense, sees beyond it to greater possibilities.

───◆───

The toughest time to make a faith confession is when everything visible is in contradiction.

When you put this verse into action, your disposition or demeanor will not be affected by what you physically see, because you know it is not permanent. Instead, you walk by faith, knowing that things are destined to change in your favor.

Power Passage Number Six: Ephesians 3:20

"Now to Him that is able to do exceedingly abundantly above all that we ask or think, according to the power that worketh in us..." (KJV).

In the Greek text, the word for think is *noeo*. It means to imagine or envision. People of faith are people who imagine bold possibilities. The truth this power passage conveys is: You cannot imagine a possibility that intimidates God. Go ahead and try it!

It is impossible to wrap our minds around what God can

do because there isn't anything He *cannot* do. Finite can never comprehend infinity. His abilities are far beyond the range of our finite thinking.

In baseball terms, if the Lord was up to bat and decided to hit a home run, we could move the back fence as far as we wanted—a thousand yards or a thousand miles, and He would hit the ball even farther!

Since this is true, the Lord is never intimidated by the amount of your faith or the size of your request. You cannot believe God for anything beyond His capacity to deliver for you.

---◆---

God is able to accomplish anything, not only by His ability but according to the power that is working in us.

"Power" is derived from the root word *dunamis*—meaning the might and muscle of God.

Just think of resurrection power. This is the same power which He demonstrated when He raised Jesus from the dead (See Ephesians 1:18-20).

Now consider this. God demonstrated dunamis (power) when He raised Jesus. This same power is at work in you and me right now. While accepting this truth requires faith, it's difficult for us to imagine. But we must believe it. "All the power that God has, is presently at work inside of me." Did you say that? Say it again, and again. Repeat it until you really believe it.

We would find it easier to believe and accept God's power working *for* us than we do God's power working *in* us.

With this much power available to you, why would you pray for such little things? Why wouldn't you expand your expectations? And why would you accept the limitations other people will attempt to place on you?

Faith begets courage, and courage leads to conquering. Ralph Waldo Emerson observed, "They conquer who believe they can."

Power Passage Number Seven: Hebrews 12:2-3

> *"[We are] fixing our eyes on Jesus, the author and perfecter of faith, who for the joy set before Him endured the cross, despising the shame, and has sat down at the right hand of the throne of God. For consider Him who has endured such hostility by sinners against Himself, so that you will not grow weary and lose heart."*

Jesus is not only the Author of our faith; He is the one who perfects and finishes it.

He is our ultimate example of how faith is to be used to endure hardships and trials. The reason Jesus could suffer such punishment and pain was because He knew what was waiting ahead in Heaven. It was the "joy set before Him" that gave Him the faith to complete His earthly assignment.

He anticipated resurrection. Actually, whenever Jesus spoke about His imminent death on the cross and the suffering associated with it, He always included resurrection in the conversation. Also, He knew a seat at His Father's right hand was the next assignment.

It is Jesus' model of perfect faith while going through severe trial that encourages us not to lose heart; but to keep the faith.

When we continually fix our eyes on Jesus, our belief, hope, trust, and expectation will be constantly strengthened.

Let me admonish you to read and re-read these Seven Power Passages until they are written on your heart. They should be heard in your talk and demonstrated in your daily walk. You're on your way to becoming a powerful person.

- By faith, Jesus focused on His promotion rather than the persecution.
- By faith, He focused on His crown rather than His cross.
- By faith, He focused on His mission rather than His misery.
- By faith, He focused on His gain rather than on His pain.
- By faith, He focused on His Father rather than His foes.
- By faith, He focused on His cause rather than His cost.

Power Key #2

Principles of Faith

Faith is a Kingdom law!

God's Word is filled with timeless truths which contain laws and principles. The same principles of faith that guided Moses when he brought the children of Israel out of bondage, worked for Peter and Paul and they will also work for you.

Some would have us believe that what happened in Bible days is not applicable in the twenty-first century. I've heard people remark, "I know what scripture says, but let me tell you about the real world."

Although the Bible is a book of history, it is not a history book. It contains principles that are just as true now as they were when written under the inspiration of the Holy Spirit. We know that *"Jesus Christ is the same yesterday and today and forever"* (Hebrews 13:8).

In truth, these are biblical times. The Bible is still speaking and it remains relevant.

There are three essential facts we need to understand concerning laws and principles:

First: A law is immutable.

The commands and ordinances of the Almighty are unchanging. God declares, *"Heaven and earth shall pass away, but My words shall not pass away"* (Mark 13:31).

The laws established by the Creator existed before man and will remain beyond him. People may challenge, doubt, question, and harshly disagree with God's laws, principles and ordinances. But the fact is, the Almighty is right—and His Word is settled. Thus, it can be trusted across the ages. *"For the Lord is good and His mercy is everlasting and His truth endures to all generations"* (Psalm 100:5).

Everything else changes; seasons, circumstances, people, the economy, administrations, regimes, and fashions. But a law established by God is an unchanging reality. Each precept can be trusted, just like the physical law of gravity. This is why the law of faith can be considered reliable by every generation. When God sees faith, He still responds in favor, which will not change.

Second: A law is irrefutable.

The principles and laws of God are impossible to disprove. Countless skeptics have tried, but all their arguments eventually fade into obscurity.

When you practice the law of faith, it will produce God-empowered results. In the process, the Lord gives you a testimony so you will be able to look back and remember what produced the outcome. Because of this evidence, you can never forget what the Lord has done for you.

From that moment forward, no one can tell you that faith doesn't work. You know the truth—and a person with an experience is never at the mercy of another's feeble argument.

―――◆―――
God also uses our faith accomplishments and achievements to silence His critics.

Our faith victories inspire others to believe, trust God, and hold onto faith during trying seasons. When people speak of the unreliability of God, we can offer proof of His faithfulness. Try refuting the law of faith with anyone who crossed the Red Sea on dry ground or with the blind man who received his sight! People tried, but here is what he said, *"One thing I know that though I was blind, now I see"* (John 9:25).

Hopefully, you have a faith achievement of your own. If not, I am praying you will.

Third: A law is indiscriminate.

The law of faith has no prejudice. It makes no difference whether you are tall, short, black, white, Methodist, or Pentecostal. Neither does it matter what part of the world you are living in. Faith works in Africa as well as Asia; in Europe and in America. The law of faith is universal. You may be surprised to know that faith works for Christians and non-Christians. You do not have to be a member of a particular church to practice this law.

"I have not seen such great faith in all of Israel." This was Jesus' statement about the Samaritan woman who came to Him with a level of faith that no one in the synagogue or church had before demonstrated.

The law of faith qualifies any person for salvation, no matter their race, gender, past failures or mistakes. It also certifies any person for all the other blessings from God. Regardless of who you are, where you are, or what you have been through, the law of faith is guaranteed to work for you. Faith in God's mercy will restore you. Faith in His grace will reposition you.

———◆———

For many, it's easy to look at past mistakes and wonder how the Lord could ever forgive and bless. But if you practice the law of faith today, it will overrule anything that happened in your yesterdays.

In the Old Testament, we read about a prostitute named Rahab who lived in Jericho. Before conquering that city, Joshua sent two men to spy it out. It was this woman who hid them in her home, protecting the men of God from certain death at the hands of the Lord's enemies.

In exchange for her act of faith and courage, the spies promised Rahab they would spare her life when they returned to conquer the city—and they kept their word. They remembered her house by the sign of a scarlet thread.

After the walls of Jericho miraculously fell and the armies of Israel marched in, the Bible explains, *"Rahab the harlot and her father's household and all she had, Joshua spared; and she has lived in the midst of Israel to this day, for she hid the messengers whom Joshua sent to spy out Jericho"* (Joshua 6:25).

---◆---

This woman, who was an outcast of society, was made dear to the heart of God by her faith.

Many are surprised to read Rahab's name in the divine lineage from David down to Christ (Matthew 1:5).

We also find her in the Hall of Faith as recorded in Hebrews 11: *"By faith Rahab the harlot did not perish along with those who were disobedient, after she had welcomed the spies in peace"* (verse 31).

Her past was blotted out and she was brought into the family of God because faith does not discriminate. Actually, it liberates and repositions even the worst of us to receive the best from the Lord.

UNCHANGING PRINCIPLES

Today, you can stand on the truth that God's laws, precepts, and covenants will never change. That includes the law of faith. It was established before the foundation of the world. Actually, according to Hebrews 11:3, God used faith to create the universe. *"By faith we understand that the universe was formed by the Word of God, so that what is seen was not made of things which are visible."*

When you apply the law of faith, the results will be so

evident that they cannot be denied.

Millions have been manipulated by the devil into believing that the reason they can't pray for a miracle is because of their behavior ten years ago, last month, or last week. Satan is a liar. Working the law of faith in the present, cancels out the predicaments of your past. You can begin obeying God right where you are.

Start practicing the powerful principles of faith that this book outlines today, and your tomorrow will amaze even you!

Power Key #3

Promises of Faith

*These are the most powerful words
either of my children can ever say to me:
"Daddy, you promised me!"*

When we have a clear insight into what God has committed Himself to do for us, it allows us to unleash our faith as never before with great confidence.

This is why knowing, believing, and speaking the promises of the Lord is so important. It obligates Him to fulfill His covenant in response to our faith and obedience.

Here is the covenant God made with Abraham: *"Go forth from your country, and from your relatives and from your father's house, to the land which I will show you; And I will make you a great nation, and I will bless you, and make your name great; And so you shall be a blessing; And I will bless those who bless you, and the one who curses you I will curse, and in you all the families of the earth will be blessed"* (Genesis 12:1-3).

This was God's promise, yet it was not automatic. After hearing from Heaven, Abraham had to respond obediently on earth. How was he able to do this? Through faith! Only through faith!

Scripture tells us, *"By faith Abraham, when he was called, obeyed by going out to a place which he was to receive for an inheritance; and he went out, not knowing where he was going"* (Hebrews 11:8).

You see, faith is "going not knowing." Any act of faith God ever calls us to will have this tagline: *"Details not included."*

Obeying the Almighty in faith will involve progressive discovery.

A Covenant-Keeping God

The Lord also promised His servant Abraham that he would be the father of many nations and that his seed would greatly multiply in the earth. One night, God took him outside his tent and told him, *"Now look toward the heavens, and count the stars, if you are able to count them...So shall your descendants be"* (Genesis 15:5).

---◆---

God's Promises are not subject to your predicament.

Sarai, Abram's wife was barren, yet God specifically promised that the two of them would be parents: *"I will bless her, and indeed I will give you a son by her. Then I will bless her, and she shall be a mother of nations; kings of peoples will come from her"* (Genesis 17:16).

In the natural, this seemed beyond the realm of possibility, especially after Abram pressed toward 100 years and his wife was apparently incapable of reproduction at age 90.

During a low moment, Sarai recommended to Abram that her maid Hagar become her surrogate. Abram impregnated Hagar, although a son was conceived, this was not God's plan and it did not fulfill His promise.

Surprisingly, God's covenant with Abram was still intact and eventually would be completed.

The Lord appeared to Abram yet again, to re-confirm His covenant promises. He also ordered him to change their names to Abraham and Sarah. And Abraham believed God.

"Without becoming weak in faith he contemplated his own body, now as good as dead since...and the deadness of Sarah's womb; yet, with respect to the promise of God, he did not waver in unbelief but grew strong in faith, giving glory to God, and being fully assured that what God had promised, He was able also to perform" (Romans 4:19-21).

What was the answer? Total, unyielding faith in God's promises.

Whatever your present deficiencies are, don't rule out what the Lord has pledged. You might be in a bad location or situation, but hold to His promises. Search the scripture to learn and understand the wonderful commitments your Heavenly Father has made to you in love. Then when it becomes necessary, say to Him, *"Daddy, you promised me!"*

Trust me. It works every time. Fathers will do anything in

their power to keep faith with their children. Remember, your Heavenly Father has all power.

"Heirs According to Promise"

The exciting truth of the story is that if you have accepted Christ by faith, you are part of this same covenant. As the Bible declares, *"Be sure that it is those who are of faith, are sons of Abraham"* (Galatians 3:7). *"Christ redeemed us from the curse of the Law...having become a curse for us...in order that in Christ Jesus the blessing of Abraham might come to the Gentiles, so that we would receive the promise of the Spirit through faith"* (Galatians 3:13-14).

Today, *"If you belong to Christ, then you are Abraham's descendants, heirs according to promise"* (Galatians 3:29).

Wouldn't you like it if your last name was Rockefeller, as in John D; or Buffet, as in Warren, or Gates, as in Bill? Any of these would be welcomed by most.

Just think about it. You are God's heir and a joint heir with Jesus Christ. The scripture tells us, *"No good thing will be withheld from you"* (Psalm 84:11). That believers are heirs by faith is a reason to praise God.

---◆---

Once we realize that everything the Lord promised Abraham we have also been promised, unlimited possibilities open up to us.

This blessed assurance makes me want to shout, *"Hallelujah!"*

A God we can Trust

We live in a world where we constantly see promises casually made and broken—and it's not just by politicians! I've had to counsel young women, who were devastated because of a broken engagement: "He told me he loved me and promised to marry me, but he didn't keep his word."

People often change their minds. But God never goes back on His vows. Today, it is unfortunate that companies and corporations are known for breaking promises made to stockholders and employees.

There are also situations when pledges made with sincere intent are unkept. Painfully I have some unkept promises on my record. How about you? This has to do with one's inability. Capacity, not character, becomes the constraint. However, it still leads to disappointment and potential disaster.

The good news is, neither of these will ever be the case with our Heavenly Father. He has both the character *and* the capacity. Everything He has ever promised, He is fully able to deliver. And He will, for His name's sake.

In the city of Antioch, the apostle Paul stood in the synagogue and proclaimed, *"We preach to you the good news of the promise made to the fathers, that God has fulfilled this promise to our children in that He raised up Jesus"* (Acts 13:32-33).

He always stands by His Word.

Never-Ending Promises

Today, you can claim what God has said for you:

- He has promised that those who believe in Christ will be saved (John 3:16; 10:27-28).

- He has promised that His grace is sufficient for us (Corinthians 12:9).

- He has promised to supply our every need (Philippians 4:19).

- He has promised His children a way to escape all temptations (1 Corinthians 10:13).

- He has promised everything that happens or does not happen for His children will turn out good (Romans 8:28).

- He has promised that by no means will He abandon us (Hebrews 13: 5-6).

- He has promised that what we give to Him, will be multiplied for us (Luke 6:38; Malachi 3:8-12).

It is only by faith that we can enter into a covenant with God and receive His blessed abundance. And don't forget these powerful words, "Daddy, you promised me!"

Power Key #4

People of Faith

*Your associations have much
to do with your achievements.*

A major reason people don't operate in faith is because they don't keep company with people of faith. Be crystal clear on this. *Your associations have much to do with your achievements.* All writers, speakers and success coaches agree on this point. Parents whatever you do, please do not ignore this principle.

If you want to become a giant in faith, your constant company cannot be midgets in faith. Men and women are either in faith or they are in fear. There is no in between. Hanging with the company of the fearful will have a negative impact on your faith pursuits. On the other hand, people of faith will impact you positively.

Hebrew 6:12 instructs us, *"That you do not be slothful (lazy), but followers of them who through faith and patience inherit the promises."*

People of faith are not lazy. We are not mere talkers, we are doers. I do not know anyone who operates in faith who shuns work. The Bible says, *"In all labor there is profit, but mere talk leads only to poverty"* (Proverbs 14:23).

People of faith are also patient. While they are working, they are waiting. They are willing to outlast any temporary setback. We will discuss this more in Part III.

Write this down and never forget it, *"What I look at and listen to will determine how I live."*

There are three categories of associations or affiliations in your life that need to be occupied with people of great faith. The three categories are companions, counselors/coaches, and co-laborers. If you will apply this power key, your life will change. In each category you must be willing to EVALUATE, ELIMINATE, AND EMULATE.

1. Companions:

The people you choose to be your close companions are vital to your future. These are friends, potential marriage mates, and those you communicate with consistently. Identify them. Who are they? Perhaps, they are what I call "your favorite five."

I suggest you write their names down and beside each answer these questions. What have they accomplished that required faith? What are they pursuing that requires faith? Do they complain and whine about circumstances, trials, and adversities? These are extremely important questions so answer them honestly. Be careful, you may learn something about yourself here!

It's amazing that we can become addicted to negative relationships. For example, you may have close companions with whom you cannot discuss your faith dream. I had been there too, until I realized that I made the choice to continue nurturing these unhealthy relationships. If you cannot share your faith dream with your friends, why are they your friends? Are they really people you need to be close to?

Friends will not envy you. They will encourage you. If they are people of faith, they will pray with you rather than poison your mind with negative ideas that breed doubt, skepticism, and low expectations.

---◆---

People in faith will motivate you to fight for your marriage, your career, ministry goals, and personal success. They want to see you win, not lose in life.

In his book, *Aspire Higher*, former NBA star Avery Johnson makes this crucial statement: "It takes five positive remarks to counter one negative one. It increases tenfold if the negative remark is made by a spouse or someone especially close to you."

Sociologists agree. When parents make negative statements to children it's next to impossible for them to overcome. If you have to be stuck for a period of time with negative companions, you must tune them out or drown them out. Do this by over–indulging in what is positive.

If you have any companions who don't pass this faith test, your challenge is to eliminate them.

2. *Counselors/Coaches (Pastor):*

Tiger Woods has a coach! Every time I think about that it humbles me. So many people will not reach their faith potential because they are unwilling to be coached or counseled by someone else.

The truth is, God built us to need others. None of us are so gifted that we can become our total best alone. We need the insight, instruction, and inspiration that someone else has to offer. Without it we cannot grow. And if we don't grow, we will not glow to the glory of God.

"Whatever I desire to be great in, I must be coached and counseled in." Yes. Write it down.

So, here is the question. Who are my faith coaches and counselors? In other words, who is the person or who are the persons from whom I am learning the principles and practices of faith? You should be able to quickly recite and list these names, and it should not be a long list—perhaps two or three names at best. You cannot listen to many voices at the same time without becoming confused.

Not just anyone should qualify to be your coach, counselor or pastor. You should choose them carefully and prayerfully. Their potential impact on your future is too significant to take lightly.

These important persons should have three things that distinguish them:

First: they should display competence.

Effective coaches and counselors must have a thorough degree of knowledge and wisdom on the subject at hand. You need someone who understands faith, can explain faith, and who teaches faith. Of course, the Bible must be their primary source, and reference book.

For them and for you, scripture has to be the ultimate authority.

Second: they should have strong character.

Your coaches and counselors should be persons of integrity who exemplify traits of godliness. But here is another aspect of character to consider. These individuals should also counsel you concerning their past mistakes as well as their successes.

It is much easier to share victories than defeats. Certainly, you want people speaking into your life who have a record of winning, both personally and professionally. However, there are no individuals who have achieved without experiencing some bumps in the road.

Every champion has had a bad season. If they are honest, they will let you see some of their scars and advise you of how to avoid the same experiences.

Third: their work should be confirmed.

Coaches and counselors should have some certification, qualification, or academic degree to confirm their range of study. In addition, when you are contemplating a faith coach or counselor, not only should they have words, they must have works of faith!

Actually, you need to be able to observe what their faith has produced. The insightful instruction they offer you should not be merely theoretical. It ought to be experiential.

I do not understand why some individuals pay so much attention to persons who are good talkers, but no works to confirm them. However, there are plenty of examples in scripture of the power of positive relationships: Moses-Joshua; Elijah-Elisha; Naomi-Ruth; Elizabeth-Mary; David-Solomon; and Paul-Timothy.

Study these and seek to model them.

3. Co-laborers:

You cannot build something truly great by yourself. You will need partners, a team, a staff, an army or supporters, but these people have to be persons of faith.

This is so critical. The agonizing burden of trying to develop or build something significant that requires faith with partners who lack faith cannot be exaggerated.

---◆---

Those you are depending on to help you accomplish dreams and build for the future have to believe what you believe, pray like you pray, and work like you work.

Conversations with them should inspire and not depress you, and drive and not drain you. In fact, you have to be able to feed off each other's faith.

You are now ready to properly evaluate your key relationships. You can use this information to assess prospective relationships as well.

The next step in the process of unleashing your faith is to eliminate the people who do not make the cut. By the way, it does not matter if they possess wonderful and admirable skill sets, knowledge, or money. Don't think any of these are substitutes for faith. Whatever people bring to the table, if they lack faith, do not stake your dream or vision on them.

Here is the exception. If you are in a relationship that you are bound to such as marriage, a ministry or otherwise, you cannot simply walk away because your co-laborers lack faith.

That would be out of order. A covenant is a covenant. So what do you do?

You unleash your faith in that situation by applying what you are learning in this book. You also pray for grace and wisdom to help those persons to become people of faith and to grow their belief and trust.

You can share books, messages, attend conferences, and of course, pray together. God will honor your faith.

As I grew in the Lord, I came to the realization that I needed to keep my eyes on people who were "movers and shakers" because of their faith—those who were demonstrating the power of their belief.

The person who is exercising faith is going to be blessed, but too often, those around them have a tendency to become jealous. So please, don't be blinded by jealousy because you cannot emulate someone you envy.

I have been there. However, I finally reached the conclusion that the people I envied continued to be favored with God's abundance. Plus, my attitude was creating a barrier that kept me from receiving valuable information and inspiration these individuals could share.

So it was *me* who was losing out and being held back—since it is impossible to envy and emulate someone at the same time.

Eliminate the zeros and embrace some heroes.

There are few individuals including ministers, business persons, entrepreneurs, and others who operate in real faith, so I decided to find a person whom I could look up to and be inspired by.

It was during this time I developed a friendship with one of the leading ministers in our city. He was someone who, when I told him my goals and aspirations, would say "Amen! You can do that and more!" He challenged and encouraged me.

I began rejoicing in everything I saw God do in this successful minister's life. I soon learned the value of the principle: "sowing where you're going."

You have to learn to bless the person who blesses you through their model, messages, and mentorship. Even this requires faith.

ONLY ONE HAD FAITH

You are in the minority when you start to walk by faith—so don't expect everyone to join you.

Following the miracle of feeding five thousand people with just five loaves and two fish near the Sea of Galilee, Jesus *"made the disciples get into the boat and go ahead of Him to the other side, while He sent the crowds away...[and] He went up on the mountain by Himself to pray"* (Matthew 14:2-23).

After the disciples were a great distance from the shore,

suddenly an angry storm erupted and the boat was being battered by dangerous waves.

There, in the middle of the night, Jesus approached the tempest-tossed boat walking on the water. When the disciples saw Him coming toward them, *"they were terrified, and said, 'It is a ghost!' And they cried out in fear"* (verse 26).

But immediately Jesus spoke to them, saying, *"Take courage, it is I; do not be afraid"* (verse 27). The Word always comes to relieve us of fear during scary moments in our lives.

Peter called out, *"Lord, if it is You, command me to come to You on the water"* (verse 28).

Jesus replied, *"Come!"*—and the Bible records how Peter got out of the boat and walked on the water toward Jesus.

Of all the twelve disciples who were on board, only one had the faith to step out onto the sea—Peter. The faithless eleven missed out on a once-in-a-lifetime opportunity.

I'm sure they thought Peter would drown. There will always be people around you who are "boat restricted." They predict the negative. Your acts of faith will reveal their faithlessness.

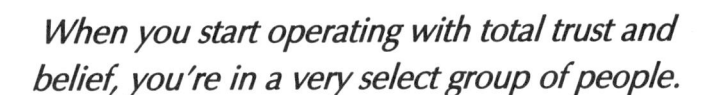

---◆---

When you start operating with total trust and belief, you're in a very select group of people.

It Can Happen for You

Start surrounding yourself with people of faith. When you see success in another person's life —whether it is a degree they have received, a career they have established, a business they have started, or a ministry they have built for the glory of God—it should inspire you to say, "Thank You Lord. If it can happen for them, it can happen for me."

Let me recommend a great book to you, *Walking By Faith* by Joe Dudley. It is the true story of Joe and his wife Eunice who built a multi-million dollar business in the hair and cosmetic industry. Just reading those pages, I could see this man and his wife walking by faith, overcoming crazy obstacles, rising above opposition, defeating adversaries, enduring incredible hardships, reaching goals, and exceeding expectations.

Find a faith hero! When you do, listen to them. Read their books and bios. Visit their locations. Walk around their facilities. Breathe the air and soak up the atmosphere, and if you can, sow something into their life. Your gift will honor God and something spiritual will happen. You will develop their spirit and before long, you will sound like those whom you admire!

Power Key #5

Practices of Faith

You cannot learn faith from someone who doesn't practice it.

One of our Power Passages says, *"...for we walk by faith, not by sight"* (2 Corinthians 5:7).

This is not a walk we choose to adopt only when it is necessary, but it must be a vital part of our daily journey. If we are not living in faith *before* problems arise, how are we going to find it when troubles multiply?

When a crisis strikes a person who is not in faith, negative reactions can vary in range and possible consequences are dangerous. They may go through a series of emotional and physical reactions: disbelief, numbness, loss of sleep, anger, irritability, loss of hope, social withdrawal, or even turn to drugs or alcohol. Often, long term problems develop over short term conditions when people are not in faith.

What a contrast to those who have the passages of faith written on their hearts and can claim the promises of God!

Living in faith enables us to quench the enemy's fiery

darts. It gives us the ability to resist the devil which causes him to flee.

A Pattern for Living

Practicing faith should be a lifestyle for believers. For example, if an opportunity presents itself today, are you ready to jump on it because you are walking in faith now? Did you leave home this morning prepared to seize any opportunity or face a challenge because you have an attitude of faith?

If this is not your pattern of living, the devil will throw you a curve ball and you won't even recognize it.

You will be limited to reacting to situations in the natural or according to your flesh. At best, this is a recipe for mediocrity. At worst, it is a recipe for disaster.

Your faith is like a garden which needs to be nurtured and watered continually—even during those times when the sun is shining and things seem to be going just fine. The way to nurture and grow your faith is to stay in the Word daily. Be diligent about hearing the Word of faith taught and preached. And make daily faith confessions that challenge you to believe and expect great things to happen.

———◆———

There should never be a day when you say, "I don't need to worry about my faith. It will be there when I need it."

FAITH THAT GROWS

Never take your faith for granted.

How do you live your daily life in light of the Gospel? You were not only saved by faith, but God expects you to be a living testimony of your belief and trust in His Son. As the apostle Paul tells us, *"your faith is being proclaimed throughout the whole world"* (Romans 1:8).

Paul wrote to the believers in Rome, *"I long to see you so that I may impart some spiritual gift to you, that you may be established; that is, that I may be encouraged together with you while among you, each of us by the other's faith, both yours and mine"* (verses 11-12).

We all have been given a *"measure of faith,"* and the Lord expects to see it grow and increase. This is why *"the righteousness of God is revealed from faith to faith"* (Romans 1:17).

Acquiring faith is not a one time experience. Rather, it is a lifetime pursuit for those who are serious about serving and pleasing God. "Without faith it is impossible to please God" (Hebrew 11:6). But according to Jesus' rebuke of His disciples, little faith also disappoints the Lord. Scripture tells us, *"The just shall live by his faith"* (Habakkuk 2:4). Therefore, we should grow our faith more and more. Our lives are dependent on it.

OUTLASTING THE DOUBTERS

Let's look again at our man Noah. When God looked down

at the wickedness in the world and decided to destroy the earth and start over, He identified one man of faith in whom He could place His total trust.

The Bible says, "*Noah found favor in the eyes of the Lord*" (Genesis 6:8). He was a *"righteous man, blameless in his time; Noah walked with God"* (verse 9).

The assignment that God gave Noah would definitely require him to unleash his faith.

You can imagine that when he told people the Lord had given him orders to build an ark (a huge ship), that would save his family and all living creatures from an impending flood, they must have thought he had lost his mind.

---◆---

A flood? It hadn't rained in years and the ground was bone dry!

The Bible tells us that Noah faithfully worked on the construction of the ark for over one hundred years. This means that decade after decade he was living his faith in front of doubters who scoffed at this aging man with a hammer and saw, constructing a boat on dry land. Of course, no water was in sight.

However, the day finally arrived when the clouds started to form in the sky, and the rain began to fall. Soon, the loudest critics were beating on the side of the ark crying, "Let me in! Let me in!" But it was too late.

Noah is confirmed and commended in scripture as a man of faith, although he looked liked a fool for a long time. He was heard day after day preaching, "It's going to rain." He was seen working diligently on a project that no one else believed in or understood. And he had no support system. He simply believed God.

Most of us are not willing to commit to and complete a work of faith because we cannot handle that degree of aloneness. We have to have the support of other people. God's Word by itself is not enough for us. However, if you need the approval of others who are not in faith, you will never unleash your faith.

Remember, *"Faith comes by hearing and hearing by the Word of God"* (Romans 10:17).

FIGHT THE GOOD FIGHT

From Genesis to Revelation we find countless men and women who demonstrated faith. Nehemiah, Esther, Ezekiel, Daniel, the disciples, and Jesus Himself are among them.

The apostle Paul, the first century missionary who wrote nearly two-thirds of the New Testament, was shipwrecked, persecuted, beaten, tortured, and imprisoned for preaching the message of Christ. Yet just before he passed from this earth, he looked back over his life and wrote, *"I have fought the good fight, I have finished the course, I have kept the faith"* (2 Timothy 4:7).

These words summarized the life of a man who believed and practiced the principles of faith as taught in God's Word.

I pray this is what you will be able to say at your life's conclusion.

POWER KEY #6

PROCESS OF FAITH

To be a partaker of God's divine nature, we begin a progression that includes <u>adding</u> qualities and characteristics until we become the person the Lord has destined us to be.

If you've ever played the game of golf you know there are a set of clubs in your bag, and each is engraved with a different number—from the driver (a 1 wood) down to a 60° sand wedge. There should be 14 clubs in your bag.

These numbers tell you how far that particular club is designed to hit the ball, and what its loft will be. For example, with the same swing and club speed, the average golfer might hit his driver (a 10-degree loft) about 250 yards and an 8-iron (a 40-degree loft) about 140 yards.

Of course, if Tiger Woods happened to be swinging the club, the ball would travel much farther!

The key to golf is to be consistent in your swing process. Then you can trust the club to do the work. The quality of your equipment certainly makes a difference. However, you could own the most expensive clubs in the world, but if you didn't know how to use them, your score wouldn't be worth mentioning.

To be really good, you must have lessons from a golf professional. It is advised that lessons are arranged periodically, because bad habits come easy but are hard to break.

GET READY FOR GREAT RESULTS

There is also a science involved in building and processing your faith.

The exact same scriptures are recorded in everybody's Bible, but the problem is that some people don't know how to use them because they have never had a personal session with a good coach or an experienced instructor. To learn faith, you need a pastor who teaches it and who rightfully divides the Word of truth.

You cannot learn faith from a person who doesn't practice it.

---◆---

God has designed His Word to do exactly what it is supposed to do. Our challenge is to practice what it teaches, never wander from the path, and watch the results.

The teachings of the Word that guide you to process faith must be ingrained in your spirit until you are able to repeat the process over and over again. Operating in faith needs to become second nature to you. In golf and other sports, this is called muscle memory. And this is what separates great golfers from good golfers.

The same formula of faith that works for small problems will also move big mountains because the process is not dependent on the magnitude of the situation.

Once you know the formula, you simply work the process. When you discover that the process really works, you gain more confidence in it.

The problem is how we tend to respond under pressure. Just like athletes, even when we know the formula, choking in a moment when the game is on the line is too common for believers. Game conditions are not for learning how. That's the time to show what you already know, especially in the big games.

Are you Adding to Your Faith?

Keep in mind that faith is just the starting point of your spiritual journey. To be a partaker of God's divine nature, we begin a progression that includes *adding* qualities and characteristics until we become the person the Lord has destined us to be.

The apostle Peter clearly spells this out as he writes, *"Add to your faith virtue; and to virtue knowledge; and to knowledge temperance; and to temperance patience; and to patience godliness; and to godliness brotherly kindness; and to brotherly kindness charity"* (2 Peter 1:5-7 KJV).

These are the building blocks, and *"as long as you practice these things, you will never stumble"* (verse 10).

The Process of Development

As we mentioned earlier, each one of us has been given *"a measure of faith"* (Romans 12:3).

But from that point forward, the process of our spiritual development begins. While we all start on the ground floor, there soon are wide variations in the amount of faith each person possesses and uses. Over time, our faith levels determine the victories we achieve, or the battles we lose.

Some have little faith.

Jesus told His disciples, not to worry about how they would find food and clothing: *"If God so clothes the grass in the field...how much more will He clothe you? You men of little faith!"* (Luke 12:28).

Worry is the pattern for too many Christians. It is made evident in the amount of sickness, disease and emotional disorders among many who claim to know the Lord.

Little faith results in worry, which leads to high blood pressure, diabetes, migraines, stomach illnesses, unhealthy weight loss and weight gain, addictions, and relational friction.

People with little faith are doubters and defeat follows them. Worry is a symptom of fear—and fear is where faith is not.

Some have great faith.

In Capernaum, a Roman centurion appealed to the Lord to heal his paralyzed servant. The man's servant was a great distance away at the time. Jesus actually offered to go home with the military officer and heal the ailing man. But the officer had great faith. He knew Jesus needed only speak the Word and the servant would be healed. He believed in Jesus' power more than His presence. He had that kind of faith. Jesus labeled it, "great faith."

The Lord marveled at this and said to those who were walking with Him, *"Truly I say to you, I have not found such great faith with anyone in Israel"* (Matthew 8:10).

———◆———

Those in great faith will experience things that are extraordinary.

Some grow *strong* in faith.

Abraham *"did not waver in unbelief but grew strong in faith, giving glory to God"* (Romans 4:20).

To grow strong in something means to increase in whatever it is—to gain more and more of it. That's what I love about the portrait the Word paints of Abraham. It depicts a man who began at one level of faith, but over time became fully persuaded in what the Lord had promised him.

That looks like me! The scripture says, "He grew strong in faith."

You can only imagine Abraham waking up one day doubting the vision and promises of God that were in his heart. "Am I a fool continuing to expect these outlandish visions and promises to come to pass? These things have never happened for anyone else, why should they happen for me?"

I'm sure these are among the questions he had to ponder. But at some point, as his faith grew, his days of doubt ended. There were no more questions and no more wavering. There was absolute certainty, even with no visible signs to support it.

As his faith matured, Abraham gave God glory. He actually praised God in faith. I believe he literally lifted his hands, opened his mouth and praised the Lord purely on the strength of the Father's promises.

Can you do that? It's a practice that will grow your faith. Begin today. Elevate your hands and voice, praising God for something He promised you. Believe you have received it. Now shout with joy while you await the manifestation!

Some are full of faith.

After the Upper Room experience and Pentecost occurred, when the church began to expand and the numbers of believers were multiplying, the Bible says, *"Stephen, full of faith and power, did great wonders and miracles among the people"* (Acts 6:8 KJV).

Amidst the many people who have some faith, there are a few who are full of faith. You should strive to be one of them. I desire that description.

A person who is full of faith will probably come across as a bit overly confident to others. Such an individual is so convinced of the things they have heard from God that their conduct and conversation never suggests anything contrary. They have full expectation of that thing coming to pass. They have a God response in the face of every challenge, situation, and circumstance. Their total worldview is shaped by the Word of God.

By the way, this kind of confidence looks like arrogance to people who don't have it.

Stephen was full of faith, grace (or favor), and power (see Acts 6:5, 8). What were the results? He did wonders and miracles among the people.

Skeptics of his day and in our time would call him a fake, a phony, and a hoax. This is what the men and women in our midst who are full of faith are called, even by Christians of weaker faith.

Remember this: Inferior faith will never produce superior works! People with lesser or no faith have difficulty recognizing those who have full faith. Simply stated, it blows their minds!

We all should pray for <u>enlarged</u> faith.

Paul encouraged a group of believers with these words: *"We ought always to give thanks to God for you, brethren, as is only fitting, because your faith is greatly enlarged, and the love of each one of you toward one another grows ever greater"* (2 Thessalonians 1:3).

An enlarged faith is one that grows more and more and more. No matter where you are on the faith scale today, by this time next month you should have more faith. How sad it is that the same things that caused some people to have panic attacks, lose their temper, fall into depression, and to faint in years past, have the same effects today. This should not be.

Enlarge your faith and you will enlarge your life!

A Process That Works

To develop a faith process that works, you must focus on different disciplines. Begin by determining your present faith level.

Answer these questions honestly.

- How have I previously responded when under duress or pressure?

- What sort of situations tend to send me over the edge?

- Does fear tend to show up in my vocabulary during a crisis?

- Who do I discuss my challenges and problems with, especially in the heat of the moment?

- Am I embarrassed by my responses to problems or conflicts after I have regained a faith perspective?

Honest answers to these questions will give you insight into where you are. Remember, the true test of faith is how you respond when you need it.

Here are some recommended disciplines that will help you develop a winning process of faith. When facing a challenging opportunity or met with a disturbing matter try these suggestions:

- Quote or read a power passage aloud. The louder and more passionate, the better. You may be in a place where only whispering is acceptable. Be in order.

- Begin thanking God immediately for a victorious outcome. Proceed to praise God for the way He is going to reveal His power, favor, and sovereignty in that situation.

- Pray for the peace of God to prevail in your mind and heart to protect you from an emotional breakdown.

- As quickly as you can, share what you are going through with someone who has a reputation of strong faith. Then listen for a faith perspective.

- Pray! Talk to the Lord, be still in His presence. The Holy Spirit will visit with you. He is our Counselor.

- Call God by His appropriate name based on the present predicament. Get a book on the names of God that defines His attributes and personality.

- Call the enemy a liar! Declare, "I will not act out of character. I am already the victor through Christ!"

When you understand and practice the process of faith, you are on your way to victory!

Power Key #7

Proof of Faith

*Be strong in the Lord and
in the strength of His might.*
– Ephesians 6:10

You can preach and teach what the Bible says from morning until night, but unless you demonstrate the principles found in the Word, your message is likely to fall on deaf ears. You can't just talk the talk, you have to walk the walk!

If you tell the world you serve a God of provision and abundance, yet there is no evidence of it in your life, ministry or business why should others listen?

We make no excuses for choosing quality and excellence—in the clothes we wear, the car we drive, the home we live in, or the people with whom we associate. Anything less would be a negative reflection on the promises God made to me. The Bible says, *"No good thing does He withhold from those who walk uprightly"* (Psalm 84:11).

The Lord desires to take us from poverty to prosperity, from sickness to health, and from the first rung on the ladder all the way to the top!

God says, *"I will make you the head and not the tail"* (Deuteronomy 28:14).

Since we have been adopted into God's family and are His heirs, we can accept His favor without apology. Please learn to expect and receive God's best with humility and gratitude, but never apologize for your faith being rewarded. Those blessings are the visible proofs of God's power to them who believe.

A Mighty Demonstration

The Lord allows you to experience miracles for a purpose. He wants you to become a living testimony of His might and power.

We can only imagine what it must have been like for the children of Israel when they were about to be overrun by the armies of Pharaoh as they camped at the edge of the Red Sea. They faced certain death.

Then God told Moses to stretch out his hand—when he obeyed, the waters parted and the Israelites crossed safely over onto dry ground. When the Egyptians chased after them, the Bible records, *"The waters returned and covered the chariots and the horsemen, even Pharaoh's entire army that had gone into the sea after them; not even one of them remained"* (Exodus 14:28).

Years later, when Joshua entered the Promised Land, he reminded the people of the *proof* of God's power they witnessed at the Red Sea— *"Your own eyes saw what I [God] did"* (Joshua 24:7).

BEYOND BELIEF!

When our daughters were younger, I told them everything I could about Disney World—Cinderella's Castle, Fantasyland, and seeing Mickey and Minnie Mouse in person. I tried to paint a picture with words, but my best efforts didn't do it justice. It wasn't until I actually took them there, that they could comprehend how exciting the Magic Kingdom really is.

―――――◆―――――
There is no substitute for personal experience.

Long ago, when King Solomon built the magnificent Temple in honor of Almighty God, the word spread throughout the known world of the splendor of this building.

The queen of Sheba heard of the Temple's grandeur. She heard of Solomon's superior wisdom and wealth and of all God had blessed him with. Thus, she eventually made the long journey to Jerusalem *"with camels carrying spices and very much gold and precious stone"* (1 Kings 10:2).

She had to see it for herself. Upon her arrival, the queen exclaimed, *"I did not believe the reports, until I came and my eyes had seen it. And behold, the half was not told me. You exceed in wisdom and prosperity the report which I heard"* (I Kings 10:7).

She saw the proof!

Absolute Evidence

The spirit of doubt is pervasive in our human nature. But some people take it to extremes, questioning and being skeptical about almost everything they hear and see.

This was also true in the time of Jesus—especially after He was raised from the dead. He appeared to Mary Magdalene and other women at the tomb (Matthew 28:1-7) and to two of the disciples on the road to Emmaus (Luke 24:13-35).

The disciples came to Thomas and exclaimed with excitement, *"We have seen the Lord!"* (John 20:25).

But doubting Thomas needed more proof. He insisted, *"Unless I see in His hands the imprint of the nails, and put my finger into the place of the nails, and put my hand into His side, I will not believe"* (John 20:25b).

Several days later, the disciples were meeting together and suddenly Jesus appeared in their midst. He walked over to Thomas and said, *"Reach here with your finger, and see My hands; and reach here your hand and put it into My side; and do not be unbelieving, but believing"* (John 20:27).

All Thomas could say was, *"My Lord and my God!"* (John 20:28). The irrefutable evidence was standing right before him, erasing all doubt.

Living Proof

If you have accepted Christ, you *know* He is alive because of how He has transformed your life.

***Now it is time to demonstrate
your conversion to the world.***

God's Word counsels, *"Prove yourselves doers of the word, and not merely hearers who delude themselves. For if anyone is a hearer of the word and not a doer, he is like a man who looks at his natural face in a mirror; for once he has looked at himself and gone away, he has immediately forgotten what kind of person he was"* (James 1:22-24).

You can't teach God's principles without practicing them, and you can't practice them without becoming living proof of His blessings and favor.

So start celebrating what the Lord has done for you. Don't forget. "God wants you to be a visible manifestation of the power of God in the presence of people."

Turn the page. You're on the way.

Part III

The Seven Power Steps to Unleashing your Faith

Introduction

The Power Keys you have been given will open wide the doors of belief, hope, and expectation. They also build a solid foundation that is essential for what you are about to discover in the second part of this book.

You have the keys, and now it is time to take the Seven Power *Steps* to unleashing your faith. This involves action —specific requirements the Lord is asking you to implement in order to move to the next level. As you take these steps to unleash your faith, you will simultaneously unlock God's power.

BEYOND THE BASICS

Transformation Precedes Transition

Unless you have mastered the basics, you are not ready for the more complex. It would be like enrolling in college without a high school education. You would quickly become discouraged and be on a fast track toward failure. So as often as is necessary revisit and re-read Part One of this book.

God has called you to be a vital member of His community of faith and to expand His Kingdom by (1) using biblical principles to guide your life, (2) building a godly home and family, and (3) sharing Christ with the world.

In the process you must allow the Lord to mold and shape you. He has a vision for your future, but you must be *willing* to yield to His plan and stay on the course He has charted.

Faith begins with believing something. But it does not stop there. It also means *doing* something. However, faith doing has to be preceded by faith thinking. That's what I mean by transformation.

Our minds, our way of thinking, has to change before our way of being changes. Our way of being must be transformed before our way of doing can change.

"As a person thinks in his heart, so is he" (Proverbs 23:7). You must think in faith in order to *be* in faith. You must be in faith in order to *do* faith. It's doing faith that changes your life! Get it? Thinking leads to being and being leads to doing.

GUIDANCE FROM ABOVE

To march forward in faith requires taking action steps. This is a law of faith based on His Word. *"Faith without works is dead"* (James 2:26).

---◆---

The wisdom and guidance we need comes only from above.

The Bible tells us, *"The mind of man plans his way, but the Lord directs his steps"* (Proverbs 16:9). And the Psalmist declares, *"Your right hand upholds me; and Your gentleness makes me great. You enlarge my steps under me, and my feet have not slipped"* (Psalm 18:35-36).

YOUR BREAKTHROUGH

There are special times in our lives when God speaks so clearly it becomes the breakthrough for which we have prayed so many years. I trust what you are reading is one of those moments. If it is, you are in store for a major *transformation* and *transition*.

Get ready to take these Seven Power Steps to unleash your faith and unlock God's power.

Power Step #1

Hearing

Faith is not a sense, nor sight, nor reason, but taking God at His Word.
— Arthur Benoni Evans

It's amazing how little the average person knows about God's Word and the message of faith it teaches—especially since the Bible is still the best selling book in the world.

How do we receive what the Lord longs for us to know? The answer is given by the apostle Paul. He quoted the words of Moses when he wrote: *"The word is near you, in your mouth and in your heart* [Deuteronomy 30:14]—*that is, the word of faith which we are preaching"* (Romans 10:8). Be saturated with scripture. You must get the Word of God down deep within you.

We know that whoever calls on the name of the Lord will be saved (verse 13), but Paul asks, *"How then will they call on Him in whom they have not believed? How will they believe in Him whom they have not heard? And how will they hear without a preacher?"* (verse 14).

After asking these questions, Paul makes this powerful statement: *"So then faith cometh by hearing, and hearing by the word of God"* (Romans 10:17 KJV).

Hearing the Word to the point of saturating your subconscious mind is a power step that must be taken seriously and acted upon literally.

If you want more faith, you must desire more hearing. Attentively listen to what the Word is saying, frequently, habitually, and reverently.

FOUR REQUIREMENTS FOR IMPROVING YOUR SPIRITUAL HEARING

According to scripture, faith does not come by seeing, thinking, feeling, or will-power. It is a direct result of hearing God's Word—and you have a vital part to play.

1. You must <u>recognize</u> the word of faith.

Many believers are too immature to distinguish whether or not what they are hearing is a real word from Heaven. As a result it makes them gullible for deception. The Bible tells us to beware of *"false teachers among you, who will secretly introduce destructive heresies"* (2 Peter 2:1).

In some instances a preacher could be a proponent of untrue doctrines, but a naive listener will think, "He's preaching the Word."

This is truly the age of itching ears spoken of in 2 Timothy 4:1-7. Too many Christians are seduced by messengers who entertain rather than teach a true and solid word. I'm amazed at much that happens in pulpits and on stages as a substitute for real Bible exposition. Many modern day "successful ministers" don't even open a Bible. And some who open and read it fail to accurately explain scripture. They only reference it.

———◆———

When you truly <u>know</u> what God has written, you will immediately recognize false doctrine.

Unfortunately, so many Christians are too lazy to read and study. Many offer the excuse they are too busy. To them I say, *"Man shall not live by bread alone but by every word God has spoken"* (Matthew 4:4).

Are you too busy or lazy to eat everyday? No excuses. Get in the Word!

Let the Holy Spirit be your teacher. He will *"guide you into all truth"* (John 16:13 KJV). Of course, His truth is His written Word.

You will instinctively know when something is wrong when you hear words spoken that do not line up with what is written.

The senses of a trained musician are immediately jarred when they hear a person singing off key, or if a piano is out of tune.

Only by immersing yourself in scripture will you be able to recognize truth from error.

Pray that God will lead you to a church that is Bible-based, Christ-centered and Spirit-filled. There, the Lord will connect you to mature Christians to help direct you in this area. But since this is critical, be sure. It *does* matter who you follow and fellowship with.

The adage is correct, "You are what you eat!"

2. You must <u>receive</u> the word of faith.

Is the soil of your heart prepared to receive the Word-seed God desires to plant in it?

To a large crowd that had gathered around Him, Jesus told the story of a farmer who sowed his seed. As he began to scatter it:

- Some fell on the road and the birds swooped down and ate it.

- Some fell in rocky places where it sprouted in the sun, but soon withered because there were insufficient roots.

- Some fell in the weeds, but the thorns grew and choked the young plants.

But the seed that fell on good soil *"yielded a crop, some a hundredfold, some sixty, and some thirty"* (Matthew 13:8).

Then Jesus compared the seed of the farmer to the Word. He explained that when anyone hears the message of the Kingdom and doesn't absorb the truth, it's like stray seed on the road—the devil swoops in and snatches it out of the person's heart.

What about the seed thrown into rocky ground? Jesus said it resembled *"the person who hears the word and immediately receives it with joy; yet he has no firm root in himself, but is only temporary, and when affliction or persecution arises because of the word, immediately he falls away"* (verses 20-21).

The seed cast in the weeds represents the individual who hears the Kingdom message, but the weeds of worry and the deceitfulness of riches strangle what was heard, and consequently, nothing grows.

Only the seed (the Word) sown in good soil—in the heart of the person who receives and understands it—will produce a bountiful harvest.

3. You must <u>respect</u> the word of faith.

I've heard ministers complain, "I wish more people would attend our midweek services or Bible studies."

Yet, in some churches, growing numbers are flocking to these services. What is the difference? When people learn that their attendance and participation is an indication of their respect and reverence for the Word, they will make the commitment to be in the house of God more consistently.

- You should respect the Word because you reverence God. If you do not respect His Word do not think you reverence Him.

- You should respect the Word because it is your #1 resource. "Man cannot live by bread alone, but by every Word that comes out of God's mouth." His Word is life to you.

- You should respect the Word because by it you make steps on an illumined path. *"Your Word is a lamp to my feet and a light to my path"* (Psalm 119:105).

———◆———

The devil works overtime to poison your mind toward ministers in general and your pastor in particular, because they are the ones who feed you the Word.

Satan will attempt to drive a wedge between you and your pastor so you will not listen to the scripture-based message being preached.

Consider these rather strong words spoken by Paul the anointed apostle to Christians at Galatia:

> *I am astonished that you are so quickly deserting him who called you in the grace of Christ and are turning to a different gospel—not that there is another one, but there are some who trouble you and want to distort the gospel of Christ. But even if we or an angel from heaven should preach to you a gospel contrary to the one we preached to you, let him be accursed. As we have said before, so now I say again: if anyone is preaching to you a gospel contrary to the one you received let him be accursed. For am I now seeking the approval of man, or of God? Or am I trying to please man? If I were still trying to please man, I would not be a servant of Christ"* (Galatians 1:6-10).

Make sure your pastor is a true and sincere Bible expositor who explains God's Word with accuracy. Then protect that relationship with prayer and discipline. Let nobody come between it. Avoid participation in destructive gossip and poisonous conversations about ministers. Such is the work of the enemy.

4. You must <u>respond</u> to the word of faith.

When you receive the message of the Gospel, something inside you will leap up and say, "This is for me!"

After the apostle Paul talked about *"the word of faith"* which he was preaching (Romans 10:8), he gave this call to action: *"If you confess with your mouth Jesus as Lord, and believe in your heart that God raised Him from the dead, you will be saved; for with the heart a person believes, resulting in righteousness, and with the mouth he confesses, resulting in salvation"* (verses 9-10).

The truth you hear originates in the Word, but it is your response that releases faith and gloriously transforms your thinking and your life. This happens as you hear and do the Word.

Never forget, principles must be practiced and then comes the result. Faith is an attitude that leads to an action. If you fail to act on the Word, it could be because you really did not believe it!

Start listening!

Power Step #2

Believing

It is cynicism and fear that freeze life; it is faith that thaws it out, releases it, sets it free.
– Harry Emerson Fosdick

After you hear God's inspired Word it must be accompanied by belief—which arises from deep within you.

When Jesus talked about mountain-moving faith, He said, *"Truly I say to you, whoever says to this mountain, 'Be taken up and cast into the sea,' and does not doubt in his heart, but believes that what he says is going to happen, it will be granted him"* (Mark 11:23).

Abraham believed God for an undiscovered country and a son when he was 100 years old.

Moses believed God would give him and his followers safe passage across the Red Sea.

Elijah believed God to send fire from Heaven on Mt. Carmel.

The woman who had been hemorrhaging for 12 years believed she could touch Jesus' garment and be made whole.

Shadrach, Meshach and Abednego believed God would

deliver them out of a fiery furnace.

Queen Esther believed God and appealed to King Ahasuerus on behalf of her people, putting her life on the line.

Robert Schuller believed God for the Crystal Cathedral although he began his ministry at an outdoor drive-in theater.

Dr. I.V. Hilliard believed God for multiple mega church locations, even when he had only 123 members.

Barack Obama believed God would lift him from the streets of Chicago helping the poor to the Presidency of the United States of America.

It is impossible to chronicle the results of "no doubt" belief, but before it becomes a reality, there are three things you must do:

1. Acknowledge the Word

It is essential that you recognize and truly confess that what God says is absolute truth.

When Philip was proclaiming the message of Christ, he met an Ethiopian eunuch, a sincere man who was reading the words of Isaiah concerning the Lamb who was led to the slaughter.

They became companions, riding in a chariot together, and Philip explained how the Lamb was Jesus and he presented the plan of salvation.

Soon, *"they came to some water and the eunuch exclaimed, 'Look! Water! What prevents me from being baptized?'"* (Acts 8:36).

Philip responded, *"If you believe with all your heart, you may"* (verse 37).

The Ethiopian answered, *"I believe that Jesus Christ is the Son of God"* (verse 37).

He eagerly acknowledged the Lord and was saved and baptized that same day.

2. Accept the Word

Many find it difficult to access the promises of God because they don't feel they are good enough to accept and receive what the Lord longs for them to have. Or, they conclude that they are not from the right family.

In the flesh we will always find reasons not to believe God for His best to happen for ourselves and those we are close to.

For example, I recently took some friends to a restaurant that was about to close for the evening. After they agreed to seat us, I remarked to the waitress, "This is going to be the best table you've had all evening"—something I often say to a waitperson.

She didn't quite know what to expect, but her level of service jumped up a few notches on pure faith that what I hinted at just might happen.

Then, when it was time to pay the bill, I was true to my word and left a tip that was almost as much as the dinner itself. She looked at the amount and asked, "Are you sure?"

The waitress found it hard to accept that kind of generosity because it so rarely happens.

Are you one of these persons who would ask God, "Are

you sure this promise is for me? Am I really to be overcome by blessings, blessed going in and going out, the head rather than the tail, going up and not down?" "Lord are you sure?" YES! He is talking to you. Just accept it!

---◆---

When the Lord opens the windows of Heaven and pours out a blessing above and beyond what you ask or think, don't feel unworthy.

Give thanks and accept it—because your Father receives joy in providing good gifts to His children.

3. Agree with the Word

Forget what others may say concerning your past, your present, or your future. Start believing and agreeing in faith with the promises of God.

On the authority of the Word, you can declare:

- "I agree that I am the head and not the tail" (Deuteronomy 28:13).

- "I agree that no weapon formed against me will prosper" (Isaiah 54:17).

- "I agree that I am more than a conqueror" (Romans 8:37).

- "I agree that I am blessed and highly favored" (Psalm 5:12).

- "I agree that when I call on God He will answer me" (Jeremiah 33:3).

- "I agree that goodness and mercy will follow me all the days of my life" (Psalm 23:6).

When you are in "one accord" with the Word, remember, all things are possible!

"Do You Believe?"

Faith and belief are not only linked, but when they are acted upon together, miracles begin to take place.

Once, Jesus was called to the home of a Jewish religious leader whose daughter had just died. The man had such complete faith that he pleaded, *"Come and lay Your hand on her, and she will live"* (Matthew 9:18). And that is exactly what happened.

Just after this incident, two blind men began crying out, *"Have mercy on us, Son of David!"* (verse 27).

Jesus asked this important question: *"Do you believe that I am able to do this?"* (verse 28).

They answered, "Yes, Lord!"

Here is the significant part of the story. Jesus touched their eyes, saying, *"It shall be done to you according to your faith"* (verse 29).

That is the question the Lord is asking concerning your

prayer for healing, a restored marriage, your business venture, your career aspirations, or your ministry vision. "Do you believe I am able to do this?"

Today, write out and speak your grand goal to the Lord. And then shout, "I believe, I know you are able to do this!"

Start activating this powerful combination in your own life—faith and belief. It will unlock God's power.

Power Step #3

SPEAKING

The words you speak, carry the authority of Heaven.

You can't keep silent when you are operating in faith. It is a divine principle that was established from the beginning.

Our world—including you and me—was created by the spoken word of the Almighty.

- *"Then God **said**, 'Let there be light'; and there was light"* (Genesis 1:3).

- *"Then God **said**,"* and the waters were separated (verse 7), vegetation sprouted (verse 11), day and night (verse 14), fish, birds, and animal life appeared (verses 20-25).

- Finally, *"Then God **said**, 'Let Us make man in Our image, according to Our likeness; and let them rule over the fish of the sea and over the birds of the sky and over the cattle and over all the earth, and over* *every creeping thing that creeps on the earth"* (verse 26).

The New Testament also confirms the role of the Word in creation. *"In the beginning was the Word and the Word was with God, and the Word was God. He was in the beginning with God. All things were made through him, and without him was not anything made that was made"* (John 1:1-3).

Because the Almighty spoke everything into creation, and *"Through faith we understand that the worlds were framed by the word of God"* (Hebrews 11:3 KJV), this means all things have the capacity to listen and respond.

Even more exciting is the fact that the Lord has given us the authority to speak on His behalf.

CONFESS, COMMAND, AND CALL

Since we are made in God's image and likeness, He has ordained that we function with the same divine power—to speak things into being. This is not presumption on our part, it is a directive from our Heavenly Father.

Be mindful that ALL speaking creates. In other words, this principle works whether the speaking is positive or negative. It works for those who are knowledgeable and for those who are unaware of it. *"Death and life are in the power of the tongue"* (Proverbs 18:21).

Most people have no intelligence on this subject. They are completely oblivious concerning what power rests in their spoken words.

You ask, "So how powerful is my tongue?" I have taught

our congregation, "Your words create your world." That is a powerful thought. Let me say it this way, "What I verbalize will materialize." This adds weight to the wise advice of thinking before you speak. Before you say it make sure you can live with it!

Ignorance is not an excuse. Every year people are killed accidentally by children playing with weapons. The child may be ignorant of how guns work but the outcome is no less the same.

So often we are guilty of wording what we are not wanting. I can certainly relate to this. Perhaps you can too. Please understand that your words do overpower your wants. So if you desire wealth you must not speak in words that coincide with poverty. For instance, "I'm broke," or "I'm poor." If you want a prosperous business or ministry, don't speak words such as, "My business will always be small," or "My church is just a little ministry."

This principle definitely needs to be applied to family, marriage, and parenting. Most people's destinies are damaged by negative words before they ever leave home. Especially at the household level your words need to match what you actually desire. This will be expanded on throughout this chapter.

There are three major ways our speaking produces the results of faith:

1. *Confessing*

Scripture gives us the formula for speaking in confession: (1) hear, (2) believe, and (3) confess. We believe only what we have heard and confess only what we believe.

Remember, the word of faith being preached *"is near you, in your mouth and in your heart"* (Romans 10:8). Then, *"If you confess with your mouth Jesus as Lord, and believe in your heart that God raised Him from the dead, you will be saved; for with the heart a person believes, resulting in righteousness, and with the mouth he confesses, resulting in salvation"* (verses 9-10).

Believing with your heart results in a righteous position—a position of favor with God. Then, when you confess with your mouth the thing you believe, it produces the outcome promised by the Word.

---◆---

If the Word stays in your heart and never gets into your mouth, it is like having money in the bank and never writing a check. It must be activated by a confession.

THE PRINCIPLES ARE TRANSFERABLE

The word "confess" in biblical Greek is "to agree with" or "to say the same thing."

This is significant because as you read God's Word, every time you come across a passage that contains a promise from the Lord to His children, stop and apply those same words to your life.

Just as you confess the Word for salvation, you also speak God's promises for every circumstance of life —economics, health, relationships, and so much more. And if you apply the same formula you will have the same results, because the principles are transferable. For example:

- If you are sick, confess: *"He was wounded for [my] transgressions, he was bruised for [my] iniquities: the chastisement of our peace was upon him; and with his stripes [I am] healed"* (Isaiah 53:5 KJV).

- If you are fearful (insecure or intimidated, confess: *"God [has] not given [me] the spirit of fear; but of power, and of love, and of a sound mind"* (2 Timothy 1:7 KJV).

- If your life is in turmoil, confess: *"The Lord is my rock, and my fortress, and my deliverer; my God...in whom I will trust"* (Psalm 18:2 KJV).

Get into agreement with the Lord! When God says He is increasing your territory, declare it verbally and tell Him, "I receive it right now."

There may be a parcel of land God is showing you to possess. By faith, claim it as yours. After all, *"The earth is the Lord's, and the fullness thereof; the world, and they that dwell therein"* (Psalm 24:1 KJV). This includes the money necessary to purchase it.

Since you have committed your ways to Him according to His Word, He has promised to give you the desires of your heart (Psalm 37:4).

THE REWARDS OF RELATIONSHIP

At the age of seventy-five, God told Abraham to leave his home, take his wife and family, and head for Canaan. When he arrived, the Lord promised, *"To your descendants I will give this land"* (Genesis 12:7).

God keeps His word. Generations later, He told Joshua, *"Every place on which the sole of your foot treads, I have given it to you, just as I spoke to Moses"* (Joshua 1:3).

This also means you! *"If you belong to Christ, then you are Abraham's descendants, heirs according to promise"* (Galatians 3:19).

Because we have been washed in the blood of the Lamb, *"The Spirit itself beareth witness with our spirit, that we are the children of God: And if children, then heirs; heirs of God, and joint-heirs with Christ"* (Romans 8:16-17 KJV).

This tells us that the promises are ours because of relationship—we receive from God exactly what Jesus receives.

Because of your position, start confessing and claiming the territory that is already yours.

2. Commanding

If you are simply praying about the situation, your formula is incomplete. Yes, Jesus tells us to pray, but then He adds another directive—*speak* the word of faith.

Jesus said, *"If you have faith and do not doubt...even if you say to this mountain, 'Be taken up and cast into the sea,' it will happen"* (Matthew 21:21).

The word "say" in this verse does not mean casual conversation. In the original Greek, it is *lego*—which means "to command." In other words you have the right to aggressively order anything that comes between you and your destiny to move out of your path.

This is not speaking figuratively, but literally.

———◆———

You issue a mandate, placing the obstacle on notice that it has to move. "Mountain, get out of my way!"

Everything Responds to a Word

A gentleman once asked me, "Pastor, do you speak to things that aren't supposed to hear?"—referring to physical objects.

"Yes! Absolutely," I replied.

"Well, how is the problem supposed to know how to move?" he wanted to know.

I explained to him that the same God who speaks to emotions speaks to the elements; the same God who commands sickness to leave commands storms to subside.

I do not feel out of place when I speak to my bank account, my home, or any other entity I possess. Since I was made in His image and likeness, I am not in faith unless I am speaking as God speaks.

The seas may be raging all around you, yet you have the

power to declare, *"Peace, be still"* (Mark 4:39). If Satan and his demons try to attack, speak to the situation. Remember, Jesus said, *"I have given you authority...over all the power of the enemy"* (Luke 10:19).

AGGRESSIVE FAITH

In the natural, some individuals or situations will not respond when we speak. They are only programmed to respond to God's voice.

This is why our words, our voice, and our authority must carry the command of the Almighty.

When we speak negatively to our obstacles and opposition, we elevate, promote and give them power over us.

Don't waste your time arguing with any person who is under your authority. Your role is to set the agenda by letting them know who is in charge.

I've seen parents try to shape the behavior of their children with everything from logic to gentle suggestions: "Don't you think it's time to clean your room?" Or, "I sure wish you wouldn't hang out with them." They do so without speaking from a position of authority.

After years of negotiating with their children, the day will come when mom or dad will give an order and it won't be heeded? Why? Because they have placed themselves beneath their own children instead of establishing and maintaining their proper role of authority.

Faith is aggressive, and you can't be timid in its operation. When you know you have the authority you don't have to apologize to anyone.

Today, take command of the situation and speak the word of faith. Remember, God did not suggest things to come into being. He commanded and they stood forth.

3. Calling

Most believers are not fully aware of the authority God has truly given them. In fact, when you read the first book of the Bible you learn that when the Creator made man and woman, He gave this directive: *"Be fruitful, and multiply, and replenish the earth, and subdue it: and have dominion over...every living thing that moveth upon the earth"* (Genesis 1:28).

Then God gave Adam the authority to name every thing He had created. Scripture tells He *"brought them to the man to see what he would call them; and whatever the man called a living creature, that was its name"* Genesis 2:10).

So when the Creator told Adam to start "calling" things, this was a signal that power was being unlocked in Heaven and transferred to man. Adam was actually walking around talking like God!

When you reflect on the situation in the Garden of Eden, there was nothing Jesus did later that Adam could not have done before He sinned. The first man had been given total authority to operate as God's agent on earth. But he forfeited that right when he listened to Satan and disobeyed the divine commands.

The reason Jesus was called "the last Adam" (1 Corinthians 15:45-47) is because He was sent to earth to fulfill the Father's original plan. And now we, as redeemed by God's Son, have been restored and returned to the place of dominion and authority we originally held.

WORDS FROM YOUR HEART

When Abraham was ninety-nine years old, the Lord appeared to him and declared, *"I will establish my covenant between Me and you, and I will multiply you exceedingly"* (Genesis 17:2). Then God said, *"No longer shall your name be called Abram, but your name shall be Abraham; for I have made you the father of a multitude of nations"* (verse 5).

This was the Almighty, calling things not as they were, but as they were going to be. At this point, Abraham and Sarah had no children together (verse 16).

God was telling Abraham that his *reality* would soon catch up with his new name which meant, "father of many nations."

This same principle applies to us today. If we speak negatively over our situation, it only fuels the problem and makes it last must longer.

---◆---

Trouble feeds on what is coming out of your mouth; it's like throwing gas on a fire.

So when your pockets are empty, if you constantly say, "I am broke," you will remain that way. And if you say,"I am sick," you are programming your body to stay in that condition—or even worse. Even when you constantly call yourself tired, you program your mind to think tired and your body shuts down under fatigue. Similarly, if you call yourself wealthy, smart, beautiful, healthy, and honorable, you will believe it and begin to become and live it.

Those things you "call"—your spoken words—are a reflection of what is taking place in your heart (mind), whether positive or negative. And what you say has consequences. As Jesus said, *"A good man out of the good treasure of his heart bringeth forth that which is good; and an evil man out of the evil treasure of his heart bringeth forth that which is evil: for of the abundance of the heart his mouth speaketh"* (Luke 6:45 KJV).

This is why the Bible counsels, *"Keep thy heart with all diligence; for out of it are the issues of life"* (Proverbs 4:23 KJV).

What do you call yourself? What do you call your spouse or your children? Must you admit that you use word labels that are contrary to what you hope to become and to what you want your loved ones to become? If so, you must accept the responsibility to change this. Believe me, this is a powerful stronghold the devil uses against us.

Remember the scriptures, "Whatever Adam called them, that was their name." When someone or something is named, that is how they are viewed by the one who does the naming. It's how they see themselves and what they answer to.

If you call (name) yourself sorry, stupid, poor, or ugly, you will live down to those labels. If you call (name) your spouse negatively, you are likely to get what you program into their subconsciousness. If you call your children dumb, thug, lazy, or other negative words, you will probably get what you say.

You may argue that you call it like you see it. Meaning if the person is acting these things out, they deserve the labels. This may be true, unless you bring in the faith perspective.

Remember, when Abram's name was changed to Abraham and Sarai was changed to Sarah, it was before they had children or even knew they could. God changed their names before their physical conditions changed.

Jesus did the same thing with Peter. His name was changed from Cephas meaning "pebble" to Peter "meaning stone of strength." Certainly in Peter's case Jesus was not basing his words on Peter's present actions. In fact, even after his name was changed Peter showed great weakness, including denying he knew the Lord while He was in custody.

It wasn't until after the crucifixion and resurrection of Jesus that the "stone" emerged. On the day of Pentecost, Peter stood and delivered a sermon in Jesus' defense. Later he went to jail for preaching Christ, but this time he did not crack under pressure. He had become the rock that Jesus had named him long before.

Maybe you and I need to begin renaming some people and some things. It is the only way for them to come forth.

POWER IN YOUR PROCLAMATION

The Lord expects to hear His children confessing,

commanding, and calling—not crying, complaining, or cursing!

Right now, let's put unleashing our faith into practice. On the authority of God's Word I can tell you:

- There is victory in your voice!
- There is a miracle in your mouth!
- There is success in your speech!
- There is triumph in your tongue!
- There is power in your proclamation.

Speak His Word!

Power Step #4

Desiring

Delight yourself in the Lord, and He will give you the desires of your heart.
— Psalm 37:4

It is my observation that most Christians are bound by an orientation or mindset that causes them to trust God for what they need, but not for what they desire. They feel like God restricts them to a standard of bare minimum.

The Lord wants us to change this way of thinking. He not only chooses to supply our basic requirements, but He wants to give us those things we dream and hope for. Our Savior spoke these words: "The thief comes to kill, steal and destroy. I have come so that you will have life, more abundantly."

After all, *"Faith is the substance of things hoped for the evidence of things not seen"* (Hebrews 11:1). Why would you hope for a substandard life, family, business, or ministry? Nobody hopes to be poor, sick, unhappy, insignificant, and unfulfilled. How is it then that so many people including Christians end up like this?

We've been taught to minimize our desires and to

maximize our needs, which is why most of our prayers are about current crisis and problems we hope God will "fix." In the process, we spend very little time asking the Lord for those things which are above and beyond our daily needs. Yet Jesus instructed, *"Whatever you desire, when you pray, believe that you have received them, and you will have them"* (Mark 11:24).

DON'T BE TIMID

Many believers seem *afraid* to have a desire, and if they do have a desire, they are reluctant to talk about it. Somehow they have reached the conclusion that God is only interested in supplying our most basic needs. Consequently, we feel selfish about asking our Father for things we want.

———◆———
God is greater than this. He is big enough to meet both our needs and our desires.

Think in terms of a parent-child relationship. Seldom does a mom or dad give their son or daughter only what they need. They usually provide much more.

When you go shopping for groceries, I'm sure you rarely buy only milk and bread. If there are kids in the house you probably purchase Popsicles®, ice cream, and perhaps a little candy. At birthdays or at Christmas, most parents do more than place a pair of shoes, socks and underwear in a gift box. The idea is to get something the child has been dreaming about—a bicycle or a video game.

Your Heavenly Father longs to treat His children the same way. Yes, He wants to meet your needs, but He takes great pleasure when He sees you rejoicing in His abundance. Deuteronomy 30:9-10 says, *"The Lord your God will make you abundantly prosperous in all the work of your hand, in the fruit of your womb and in the fruit of your cattle and in the fruit of your ground. For the Lord will again take delight in prospering you, as he took delight in your fathers, when you obey the voice of the Lord your God, to keep his commandments and his statues that are written in this Book of the Law, when you turn to the Lord your God with all your heart and with all your soul."*

THERE ARE REQUIREMENTS

Jesus tells us, *"Ask, and it will be given to you; seek, and you will find; knock, and it will be opened to you"* (Luke 11:9).

If you are using your faith only to have your utility bills and your car note paid, this is all you are going to receive. But God's will is to give you much more, and He doesn't mind hearing your "wish list."

Again, the Bible says, *"Delight yourself in the Lord; and He will give you the desires of your heart"* (Psalm 37:4). A light bill most likely does not fit that description.

However, if you read the next verse you'll find there are two requirements involved to receive what you request: (1) commitment and (2) trust. "Commit *your way to the Lord, trust also in Him, and He will do it"* (verse 5). This has to do with obeying God, living in His will, and activating promises by following biblical principles.

God promises to respond to your desires, but there is a principle and a procedure involved.

First: Identify what you desire.

Be specific and clear regarding what you are asking the Lord for. You can't be "wishy-washy!"

The word "desire" in biblical Greek is *aiteo*—meaning "to ask repeatedly, almost demanding."

I can tell you from personal experience that when a child wants something badly enough they begin by testing the waters, letting you know what it is. If you react with a, "No," they will come back with a pitiful look on their face and ask again. If they still don't get the right answer, they may start nagging you by questioning, "Well, when can I have it?"

My wife and I are often amazed at the persistence of our children. They have proven their confidence in the power of persistent asking. They can ask the fourth time as if they don't recall the prior three unfavorable responses. It is hard to convince them that we really meant "No," especially when they know we are able to grant their request.

Often, they eventually wear you down and you find yourself giving in. Perhaps while shopping, you too have thrown something into the cart you really didn't want to buy, just to satisfy your child's longing.

I know this may sound foreign to many, but there are some things God wants you to *require* Him to do—to put pressure on Him according to your faith in His ability and awareness of His Fatherly favor towards you.

When you have identified the object of your desire and settled on it, don't give up. This may mean reminding the Lord, "I'm asking for the same thing this year I wanted last year. I haven't changed my mind. In fact, I desire it even more."

---◆---

Stay on your knees until you hear from Heaven. Unless God says, "No" then the answer may be "Not Yet."

Second: Qualify the object of your desire.

Since God has parameters, what you are requesting must pass a test:

- It must not be hurtful to other people.
- It must not be harmful to yourself.
- It must not be dishonoring to God.
- It must not be adverse to God's purpose.
- It must not be in conflict with His Word.

It makes no sense for the Lord to bless you with something that causes harm.

Would you give a ten-year-old the keys to your car? Of course, not! The risk would be too great. Suppose you did and the kid had a wreck and fatally injured someone. You should expect to be charged with the persons death.

On our spiritual journey, the Lord will withhold giving

certain things until He thinks we are ready.

---◆---

God isn't saying, "No," He is saying "Grow" —waiting for us to reach a certain level of maturity.

Some may ask the Lord for a degree of prosperity they really can't handle. If received prematurely, they would spend the money frivolously and forget to attend the house of God.

The deeper you develop in faith and godliness, the more the Lord will trust you with the desires of your heart.

Once your request passes His test—and you pass the maturity test—the Lord is more than able and willing to bless you.

WATCH YOUR WALK

God's response to your desires is based on whether or not you are walking according to His principles and precepts. As David writes, *"No good thing does He withhold from those who walk uprightly"* (Psalm 84:11).

Too often, it is the "uprightly" part that creates the barrier for us. Check your life frequently. Make sure you are growing spiritually and not just asking God to bless you materially.

For this reason, my daily meditation includes passages such as Deuteronomy 28 and Psalm 119. Every day, I want to see my life through the light of God's word.

The Lord increases favor in response to our faithfulness.

Power Step #5

Praying

*Prayer is like the turning on of an
electric switch. It does not create the current;
it simply provides a channel through which
the electric current may flow.*
–Max Handel

Prayer is an essential step in unleashing our faith and unlocking God's power. It is person-to-person communication with the Almighty, and when we fail to exercise this privilege we either treat God like He is not a Person or as if He is *unnecessary*.

Some people pray and are only heard by human ears. Yet others pray and heaven is moved to action.

I think now of three men in particular whose prayers moved Heaven to action. The first is my late grandfather, the Rev. C.D. Dixon. Early every morning, he met with God in the tiny and only restroom in his humble dwelling. He prayed there with such fervor that nobody dared to interrupt him. We knew that any interruptions would have interrupted *them*—we were sure God was in that tiny space with him.

Two over prayer movers are Drs. S.J. Gilbert, Sr. and William A. Lawson, two sages in the ministry. When they pray, you get the sense that the Lord is listening attentively.

———◆———

Prayer is an acknowledgment of our utter deficiency and God's total sufficiency.

Through our neglect to pray, the Lord is disrespected.

Since scripture tells us that God is our Father, if we don't pray, we are ignoring the One who is responsible for bringing us into this world and into the Kingdom. Our Heavenly Father is not just an entity but the most *necessary* Person in our lives. Talk to Him.

Is It Your Priority?

To pray in a time of peace as passionately as I do in a time of panic....that's my goal.

Many Christians have friends they talk to every day—some more than once. Yet, they can go weeks without ever talking with the Lord.

Since God is the most important Person in my life, I begin each day by talking to Him first. Rarely do I even talk with my wife until I have had a conversation with the Lord.

Typically, we *both* pray before we start conversing with each other. In our list of priorities, God is Number One and our relationship is second.

This fellowship with the Lord tempers my spirit, prepares my heart, and gives me the right perspective to face the world.

Spending time in God's presence is essential and should not be limited to just an early morning prayer or the last thing you do at night. 1 Thessalonians 5:17 reads, *"Pray without ceasing."*

---◆---

Throughout the day, take time to pause, even if only for a moment, to have a conversation with the Lord. Ask Him for hourly guidance, wisdom and power.

WHAT DOES PRAYER EXPRESS?

Prayer is much more than knocking on the door of Heaven with our list of needs. The fellowship we share with our Heavenly Father communicates four things:

First: Prayer expresses our desire for God.

An amazing reaction takes place when you drink water; your body will ask for more! It's the same with God. Just as your physical being craves an extra dose of what you give it, when you pray, your soul desires more and more of the Lord. *"As the deer pants for the river brooks, so my soul thirsts for God, for the living God"* (Psalm 42:1-2).

2. Prayer expresses our devotion to God.

In church we often sing, "I Surrender All," but do we truly

mean these words? Does our prayer life reflect total dedication to the Lord?

When we pray frequently we remain devoted to Him. Pleasing Him becomes the greatest of our desires. His glory becomes our goal.

Our communion and daily fellowship is a direct reflection of the intensity and passion we have for God.

3. Prayer expresses our delight in Him.

When you speak to another person consistently and voluntarily, it usually indicates you are pleased with them.

You should not wait until fear and circumstances force you to speak to God and ask for His help. Initiate intimate conversation and tell the Lord, *"In Your presence is fullness of joy; in Your right hand there are pleasures forever"* (Psalm 16:11).

Learn to enjoy your moments with Him. When you do, you will guard that time because it's precious and priceless.

4. Prayer expresses our dependence on God.

When you fail to pray, you slight the Lord by indicating, "I can do this without You. I can have my spouse, family, career, or build a great ministry on my own."

The Lord just smiles and allows you to go right ahead and try, knowing you will finally realize how incapable you are in your own strength.

Children love to say, "I can do it all by myself," and at times we let our kids break something or fail at something to teach them a lesson. This helps them understand that when we offer our assistance or wisdom, it's for their own good.

God knows our limitations and we should be aware that *"Pride goes before destruction, and a haughty spirit before stumbling"* (Proverbs 16:18).

We must daily express our dependence on Him.

IT'S ALREADY YOURS

What can we pray for? God's Word says, *"all things"* (Mark 11:24). This is an unlimited category, and "whatsoever" means we are to fill in the blanks. Of course, remember the earlier lessons on qualifying our desires and obeying the Word.

———◆———

A healing in your family? A promotion in your job? The Lord is waiting for you to ask Him.

When you utter the prayer of faith, take Jesus at His word when He tells you, *"believe that you have received them"* (verse 24).

This takes us to a new dimension because we've been trained to think that the answer to our prayer is a "future" event. But according to the Word, when you pray, believe the work is already completed—that you *"have received"* the answer. It is then a past event, even though it may manifest in the future.

For example, if you are praying for your life's mate, describe the person you are hoping for in detail. Then tell

God, "I come to You in the name of Jesus, based on the promise of Your Word. I believe you have already picked out this special person and he (or she) is mine. In Your perfect timing You will allow our paths to cross."

Then let the Lord know, "I am giving you the praise and glory for what you have already done." Use the same process for every other expectation.

Perhaps you have been smoking for thirty years and are anxious to overcome the addiction to nicotine. Pray, "Lord, I know this is not the will of God for my life or for my body. Father, I am asking you to remove this toxic habit from me." Then begin to declare, "I have the power to overcome it. I am no longer a smoker. I am free in Jesus' name!"

Receive this by faith, claim it in the name of Jesus, and proclaim to the world cigarettes are no longer a part of your lifestyle. Immediately or eventually you will gain power to resist smoking. The flow of God's power will cause your desire to change.

In the words of the French theologian, Francois Fenelon, "He who prays without confidence cannot hope his prayers will be granted."

THANK HIM IN ADVANCE

I remember the car commercial with someone jumping in the air, clicking his heels, and singing, "Oh, what a feeling. Toyota!"

In the process of faith, you receive the thrill once you *ask and believe* because this is when you receive it—even before you have the manifestation, answer, or evidence. So start rejoicing in the new reality. This takes real discipline.

> *Most people praise God for the blessings they can see and touch, but when, by faith you receive something in advance, it changes your prayer life.*

The Bible admonishes us, *"Be anxious for nothing, but in everything by prayer and supplication with thanksgiving let your requests be made known to God"* (Philippians 4:6).

Why would I thank the Lord for something I don't have? Because I believe I have already received it!

If you are anxious to move out of an apartment and become a homeowner, pray, "Lord, I claim my house and believe you have arranged everything possible to make this a reality." Then every day, pray, praise, and pursue! Pray, praise, and pursue! Pray, praise, and pursue!

Pursuing means to practice what you are praying. You cannot pray in love and practice hate. Or, pray for mercy and practice unforgiveness. Or, pray for God's bounty and practice selfishness. Or, pray for success and practice slothfulness. Don't be guilty of saying great prayers with your words then rising to *un-pray* them with contrary works.

The day will come when you will not only pray, praise, and pursue. You will eventually possess!

When God sees this kind of faith, He assigns angels to start working things out on your behalf. He says, "My child keeps praying and praising me for what he or she desires. Pick out the builder. Tell his boss to give him a raise. Do whatever is necessary to bring it to pass. The Lord delights in this level of faith.

POWER STEP #6

WORKING

The faith of the head is faith that is dead;
The faith of the heart is better in part;
But the faith of the hand is the faith that will stand,
For the faith that will do must include the first two.
– Anonymous

The missing ingredient in most people's formula for success is a four letter word called W-O-R-K!

In our society, work is defined as a set of coordinated and concentrated actions that are designed to accomplish a pre-determined objective.

We love to quote Jesus' saying, *"If you have faith…nothing will be impossible for you"* (Matthew 17:20). But we are less enthusiastic about using the scripture, *"faith without works is dead"* (James 2:26).

Let me give you insight on how this process of faith produces results. We have looked at the following verses individually, but here is how they are linked together.

We know that *"Faith is the substance of things hoped for,*

the evidence of things not seen" (Hebrews 11:1 KJV), but how do we receive it? *"Faith cometh by hearing, and hearing by the word of God"* (Romans 10:17 KJV).

Next, we activate our faith by believing and speaking: *"What things soever ye desire, when ye pray, believe that ye receive them, and ye shall have them"* (Mark 11:24 KJV). *"The word is near you, in your mouth and in your heart—that is, the word of faith"* (Romans 10:8).

When this is combined with desire (Psalm 37:4-5) and prayer (Philippians 4:6), we are ready for a *work* of faith, which corresponds to the *word* of faith.

The apostle Paul told the believers at Thessalonica, *"We give thanks to God always for all of you, making mention of you in our prayers; constantly bearing in mind your work of faith and labor of love and steadfastness of hope in our Lord Jesus Christ in the presence of our God and Father"* (1 Thessalonians 1:2-3).

A POWERFUL COMBINATION

Faith is an act of rational choice which determines us to act as if certain things were true and in confident expectation that they will prove to be true.
– William R. Inge

From Genesis to Revelation, the Lord gives us examples of individuals who were filled with belief, hope, and spiritual expectation, yet they still put their hand to the plow:

- *Noah combined faith and works.*
  He believed God had chosen him for a special purpose and spent 120 years building the ark (Genesis 6).

- *Joseph combined faith and works.*
  After being sold into slavery and placed in prison, God used Joseph to save His people (the Jews) from famine and he became the governor of Egypt (Genesis 37-47).

- *David combined faith and works.*
  From toiling in the fields as a shepherd to becoming King Saul's armor bearer, God was preparing David for the throne (1 Samuel 16).

- *Nehemiah combined faith and works.*
  When the Lord told Nehemiah to rebuild the walls of Jerusalem, he declared, *"The God of heaven will give us success; therefore we His servants will arise and build"* (Nehemiah 2:20).

- *Jesus combined faith and works.*
  The Son of God said, *"I must be about my Father's business"* (Luke 2:49 KJV). He was here to *"do the will of Him who sent Me and to accomplish His work"* (John 4:34).

- *The followers of Christ combined faith and works.*
  Matthew was a tax collector.
  Luke was a physician.

Peter was a fisherman.
Paul was a tentmaker.

In the final chapter of the last book of the Bible, Jesus is saying to you and me, *"Behold, I come quickly; and my reward is with me, to give every man according as his work shall be"* (Revelation 22:12).

How Faith Comes Alive

The apostle James gives us a full explanation of how faith and works are both part of God's plan and how they are valuable in our Christian walk:

> *What use is it, my brethren, if someone says he has faith but he has no works? Can that faith save him? If a brother or sister is without clothing and in need of daily food, and one of you says to them, "Go in peace, be warmed and be filled," and yet you do not give them what is necessary for their body, what use is that?*
> *Even so faith, if it has no works, is dead, being by itself. But someone may well say, "You have faith and I have works; show me your faith without the works, and I will show you my faith by my works."*
> *You believe that God is one You do well; the demons also believe, and shudder. But are you willing to recognize, you foolish fellow, that faith without works is useless?*
> *Was not Abraham our father justified by works when he offered up Isaac his son on the altar? You see*

that faith was working with his works, and as a result of the works, faith was perfected; and the Scripture was fulfilled which says, "And Abraham believed God, and it was reckoned to him as righteousness," and he was called the friend of God.

You see that a man is justified by works and not by faith alone. In the same way, was not Rahab the harlot also justified by works when she received the messengers and sent them out by another way?

For just as the body without the spirit is dead, so also faith without works is dead (James 2:14-26).

GIVE GOD SOMETHING TO BLESS

I've met people who covet the position of their boss and the increased income it would bring. But they aren't prepared for the sacrifice it takes to earn the credentials for the job or the long hours involved to handle the added responsibility.

Stop for a moment and ask yourself, "What is the vision God has placed within me regarding my future?"

Perhaps you will see a picture of yourself in a cap and gown, walking across the platform of a major university with a diploma in your hand.

―――◆―――

The Lord places dreams within you to motivate and inspire you to begin the years of work and countless hours of study it will take to make the vision a reality.

Maybe the Lord is showing you an enterprise He wants you to launch. This means that as you step out in faith you will need to master every aspect of the operation—including developing a marketing plan, raising capital, and providing the goods or services to exceed expectations.

In short: you must learn to love work. Why? The Lord cannot bless your "nothing," but He will bless your "something."

NIGHT IS COMING!

Yes, I believe that Jesus is returning soon to carry His bride away, but this doesn't mean we should become lazy Christians and sit idly by until the rapture. No, we are to live by the command, *"Occupy till I come"* (Luke 19:13).

Jesus said, *"I must work the works of Him who sent Me as long as it is day; night is coming when no one can work"* (John 9:4).

When your faith and your works become one, you will be a living testimony of the promises of God.

Power Step #7

Waiting

The great believers have been unwearied waiters.
  - Anonymous

The final and most challenging step in unleashing our faith is waiting on the Lord to fulfill His promise. Often people who begin in faith become discouraged by delays, detours and disappointments. When they do, they cease to exercise faith by giving up on the other keys and steps. They stop doing the things that keep you in faith. But people of great faith simply won't quit! They don't give up because they keep believing.

Yes, we believe and confess, but for some, if the Lord doesn't move immediately, doubt sets in and they take three steps back.

The Road Called "Delay"

If we are not aware of how the Lord works, the time it takes before seeing the results can cause three human reactions:

1. Delay can lead to Doubt

We don't question God's ability when we first call on Him in prayer, but after a month or two goes by, questions surface that can even *replace* our faith. When there is no answer, we stop believing, speaking, and commanding and working, because we become apprehensive. We think, "If this is not going to happen I don't want to be let down." Nor do we want to be embarrassed—so we no longer discuss the issue.

But this is not the Lord's plan.

Since God's timetable is not ours we must *"ask in faith without any doubting, for the one who doubts is like the surf of the sea, driven and tossed by the wind"* (James 1:6).

Faith has to be supported by trust. Faith is knowing God can and believing He will. Trust is accepting His way and His timing.

2. Delay can lead to Dabbling

God told Abraham and Sarah they would have a son, but when she remained barren, Sarah decided, "We have to take matters into our own hands."

Because the evidence of God's promise did not come soon enough, they decided to use their own ingenuity —dabbling in a matter they should have left exclusively to the Lord. Please do not miss this.

Sarah was beyond childbearing years and became

emotionally frustrated. So she devised a plan for her Egyptian servant, Hagar, to bear a son with Abraham, She told him, *"The Lord has prevented me from bearing children. Please go in to my maid; perhaps I will obtain children through her"* (Genesis 16:2).

Like Sarah, there are times we lose heart during this vital stage of waiting on God.

Remember these words by George MacDonald in his book, *Weighed and Wanting: "The principle part of faith is patience."*

When Hagar conceived, Sarah immediately became extremely jealous of her, and this caused great dissension in the household. In fact, Sarah treated her maidservant so harshly that the woman fled from her presence (verse 6).

An angel of the Lord found Hagar sitting near a well in the desert and told her to return to Sarah. She did, and a son was born named Ishmael—but this was not the child God promised would be conceived by Sarah.

———◆———

When you get ahead of the Almighty, trying to rush His divine plan, there is nothing but trouble ahead.

3. Delay can lead to Division and Depression

Several years later the true son of Abraham and Sarah was born. His name was Isaac.

During a great feast to celebrate the weaning of the child, Sarah witnessed Ishmael (thirteen years old at the time) mocking young Isaac. Upset, she told Abraham, *"Drive out this maid and her son, for the son of this maid shall not be an heir with my son Isaac"* (Genesis 21:10).

The next morning, Abraham reluctantly sent Hagar and Ishmael away, giving them some provisions of bread and water for their journey. They left the safety and security of Abraham's household and wandered about in the wilderness of Beersheba.

Scripture records how when their supplies were gone, *"She left the boy under one of the bushes. Then she went and sat down opposite him, about a bowshot away [and] said, 'Do not let me see the boy die.' And she sat opposite him, and lifted up her voice and wept"* (verses 15-16).

Hagar sank into a state of total depression. But remember, the seeds of this problem were planted long before when Sarah wouldn't wait on God's timing to deliver a promised son.

Perhaps you have been engulfed in a situation where there was nothing left but lost hope, and you thought God had forgotten all about you. Your plight may have been so painful that you felt yourself slipping into despair.

However, even at your lowest point, God is still watching over you.

Thankfully, the Lord heard the crying of Hagar and Ishmael. An angel called from Heaven, saying, *"What is the matter with you, Hagar? Do not fear, for God has heard the voice of the lad where he is. Lift him up and take him by the hand, for I will make him into a great nation"* (verses 17-18).

When she opened her eyes, there was a well of water and the two of them drank their fill and survived.

WHAT FAILING TO WAIT REVEALS

Since faith is defined as an uncompromising confidence in God's ability to perform His perfect will on our behalf, no matter who or what the opposition, waiting is a profound expression of this confidence. Hebrews 11:1 states, *"Now faith is the substance of things hoped for, the evidence of things not seen."*

The inability for people to wait on God to do His work unmasks two character flaws:

First: It reveals Immaturity

If you tell a child you are going to buy them some ice cream, they want you to stop whatever you are doing so they can have it that very moment. Or you load the car for a long road trip to grandma's or a vacation destination and twenty minutes later you hear, "Are we there yet?" Not even a two and a half hour flight to Orlando, the land of Disney, is quick enough for our children!

When children grow older, however, they begin to learn they can't have everything "right now."

Sadly, many adults are still at a level of immaturity in their faith. They link God to our world of fast foods, quick fixes, and instant messaging.

But the Lord says, "I know where I am taking you, just give Me time to get you there."

Paul says, "When I was a child, I spoke as a child and thought as a child. But when I became a man (mature), I ceased with childish behavior." Get it? Impatience reveals immaturity. Rather than whining we should be patiently waiting.

Too many people are so easily blown around by winds of adversity and challenge. As soon as they see or experience anything that conflicts with what they desire or seek, they start to doubt. They become a flustered bundle of nerves and respond emotionally.

Second: It reveals Instability

When you are not firmly rooted in your faith, the slightest breeze can steer you off course.

James tells us that the person who operates in doubt rather than faith *"ought not to expect that he will receive anything from the Lord, being a double-minded man, unstable in all his ways"* (James 1:7-8).

CHANGE IS COMING!

As we are waiting on God in faith we must learn to handle

the passing of time.

Job was a righteous man, but the Lord allowed Satan to test his faith. At the lowest ebb of his life he asked, *"If a man dies, will he live again? All the days of my struggle I will wait until my change comes"* (Job 14:14). This is the person who declared, *"Though he slay me, yet will I trust in him"* (Job 13:15 KJV).

Job was admitting, "God could deliver me today, next week, or next year, but I'll be right here—hoping, trusting, waiting, and believing that my time is going to come." And it did. The day finally arrived when the test of his faith was over, and *"The Lord blessed the latter days of Job more than his beginning"* (Job 42:12).

God was watching over him, and Job received a double portion of everything he had previously lost.

Divine Expectation

The best prescription for despair is hope. It is what gives you the ability to believe, "Sooner or later, my blessing is going to arrive. Any day now it's going to happen for me."

With divine expectation you can be assured, "The seed I sowed last month is going to produce a harvest."

———◆———

Remember this: you cannot wait without hoping—and you cannot hope without waiting.

The ability to look ahead with positive anticipation is rooted in scripture. David asked, *"Why are you in despair, O my soul? And why have you become disturbed within me? Hope in God, for I shall again praise Him"* (Psalm 42:5).

His expectation, however, wasn't necessarily for an immediate answer. David's adversaries were hot on his heels and almost had him in their grasp, but he was able to declare, *"I will hope <u>continually</u>, and will praise You yet more and more"* (Psalm 71:14).

---◆---

Waiting for an answer from the Lord doesn't mean your are to be lazy or stay silent. Just the opposite, it's the time to lift your praise to another dimension.

Praising Fuels Your Patience!

When you are going through the valley, instead of being despondent and dejected, stand to your feet and begin praising God—and give Him the glory with greater intensity than ever before.

Two Preparations

Waiting is not idle time, neither is it passive in nature. During this season God is *preparing* and equipping us for what is about to happen.

While you are waiting, two things are taking place in the Heavenly realm:

One: God is preparing you.

The Lord is getting you ready for a marvelous blessing! The Hebrew word in this context is *chalats*, meaning "to pull off, strip, or to equip for battle."

God knows what you are praying for, and when He agrees with you, He says, "What will I do to make sure My child is ready?" So He strips away any unnecessary layers.

This is much like a soldier who enlists in the Army. The day he reaches boot camp, he is given a military haircut to strip him of his civilian mentality, and is called by a number instead of a name. Next, the rigorous physical training begins and he learns to obey orders without asking why. All this is to prepare him for the battlefield.

When a soldier returns home from boot camp, he is a changed person both mentally and physically. His muscles are a little more toned and defined, he walks taller, and carries an air of confidence.

God knows that greater blessings lead to greater burdens. When we are elevated by God the enemies' attacks will become fiercer. So, since God sees the battle after the blessing, He patiently grooms us not just for the blessing but for the enemies' response to our elevation.

Similarly, you are also being prepared in God's army, and training is required. The Lord is about to do something amazing for you, but you are going to have to fight to obtain it, and fight to hold on.

---◆---

*God continues working on you until
He believes you are ready.*

The Lord wants to make sure you are fit for your station in life. He doesn't want you to be embarrassed, or to look as if you don't belong.

Another Hebrew word for "prepare" is *kuwn:* to stand erect and be established.

The children of Israel were headed for the Promised Land, but first they had to go through the wilderness—and many fell by the wayside because they failed to obey and did not meet God's standards.

Of the twelve spies sent by Moses to check out Canaan, only two, Joshua and Caleb, returned with a positive report—and they were the ones whom God felt were equipped to lead His people into the land.

Two: *God is preparing the blessing.*

The Lord is not only getting you ready for tomorrow, He is also at work—planning and making preparations to pour out His abundance.

David writes, *"You prepare a table before me in the presence of my enemies"* (Psalm 23:5). The word "prepare" means the Lord is arranging everything and setting it in place.

We are impatient and want to sit at the banquet table this very moment, but God says, "When the time is right, I will usher you into My presence and give you a special seat." Why sit at the table pouting while God is preparing?

Praise the Lord! He is putting all things together for our good.

Waiting in Faith

When Jesus was about to ascend into Heaven and return to His father, the disciples and those who loved Him were greatly concerned for their future. What would happen when He was no longer walking with them?

His answer involved waiting. Jesus gathered His followers together and told them not to leave Jerusalem, *"but to wait for what the Father had promised"* (Acts 1:4)—speaking of the Holy Spirit who would descend upon them.

It's only natural for people to be anxious and restless, and the believers also wanted to know when Israel would be restored, But Jesus told them, *"It is not for you to know the times or the seasons, which the Father hath put in his own power. But ye shall receive power, after that the Holy Ghost is come upon you; and ye shall be witnesses unto me both in Jerusalem, and in all Judaea, and in Samaria, and unto the uttermost part of the earth"* (verses 7-8).

These are the last words Jesus spoke on earth before He ascended to Heaven. I think it is significant that He mentioned we will not know *"the times or the seasons."* This rests in God's hands.

Say this aloud over and over again, "Times and seasons are God's business; not mine."

Our directive is to wait with faith. *"Let us hold fast the confession of our hope without wavering, for He who promised is faithful"* (Hebrews 10:23). *"For we have become partakers of Christ, if we hold fast the beginning of our assurance firm until the end"* (Hebrews 3:14).

No man knows the day nor the hour when Christ will return, but we know He is coming soon.

YOUR COMMITMENT AND DECLARATION

It is my prayer that as a result of what we have shared together, your spiritual life will take a giant leap forward.

Starting today, begin to use the Seven Power Keys of Faith. I am asking you to make this commitment:

1. "I will read and study the PASSAGES of faith."
2. "I will apply the PRINCIPLES of faith."
3. "I will claim the PROMISES of faith."
4. "I will surround myself with PEOPLE of faith."
5. "I will live by the PRACTICES of faith."
6. "I will follow the PROCESS of faith."
7. "I will demonstrate the PROOF OF THE POWER of faith."

In addition, make a declaration that you are walking in the Seven Power Steps of Faith:

1. "I am HEARING the message of faith."
2. "I am BELIEVING the God of faith."
3. "I am SPEAKING the words of faith."
4. "I am DESIRING the results of faith."
5. "I am PRAYING the prayer of faith."
6 "I am WORKING the works of faith."
7. "I am WAITING for the blessings of faith."

By using these essential keys and taking these required steps, you will Unleash Your Faith and Unlock God's Power!

Notes

FOR ADDITIONAL RESOURCES
OR TO SCHEDULE THE AUTHOR TO EDUCATE,
MOTIVATE, TEACH OR PREACH, CONTACT:

JAMES DIXON, II
P.O. BOX 924083
HOUSTON, TX 77292

PHONE: 888-650-7258
EMAIL: jd2@clearsail.net